D0095164

Small Library Cataloging

Third Edition

Herbert H. Hoffman

The Scarecrow Press, Inc.
Lanham, Maryland, and London
2002

SCARECROW PRESS, INC.

Published in the United States of America
by Scarecrow Press, Inc.
4720 Boston Way, Lanham, Maryland 20706
www.scarecrowpress.com

4 Pleydell Gardens, Folkestone
Kent CT20 2DN, England

British Library Cataloguing in Publication Information Available

Library of Congress Cataloging-in-Publication Data
Hoffman, Herbert H.
      Small library cataloging / Herbert H. Hoffman.—3rd ed.
      p. cm.
      ISBN 0-8108-3730-7 (alk. paper)
          1. Cataloging. 2. Classification—Books. 3. Small libraries. I. Title.
      Z693 .H64 2002
      025.3—dc21   Library of Congress Control Number: 2001041791

1st ed. 1977 by Headway Publications, ISBN 0-8953-7003-4
2nd ed. 1986 by Scarecrow Press, ISBN 0-8108-1910-4

Contents

Preface

This book was primarily written for all who find themselves in charge of a small library without having had the benefit of formal instruction in library cataloging. The book attempts to simplify cataloging in small libraries, but it offers no facile oversimplifications. It does not insult the dedicated layperson's intelligence by pretending that cataloging is easy.

Libraries, even small libraries, are astonishingly complex organizations. There is a proliferation of media. There are monographs and series and serials, regular and irregular. There are personal authors, editors, performers, translators, and corporate authors, books that have one or several authors, natural titles and uniform titles, stand-alone works, collections, anthologies, and myriad other variables. Library catalogs are complicated structures. There are entry principles and headings, added entries, open entries, closed entries, and analytical entries, simple and complex subject headings, genre and form headings, tracings, cross references, location codes, shelf lists, authority files, and much more.

The *Anglo-American Cataloguing Rules* published under the auspices of the American Library Association (ALA) fill a thick book. Several books explaining these rules have been written. It is safe to say that cataloging remains a specialty mastered by few, even among librarians with professional degrees. Needless to say, the volunteering or appointed layperson cannot be expected to catch up with this growing body of esoteric knowledge in a few easy lessons. Nor does he or she need to. I claim that the cataloging of small libraries can safely be simplified.

To this end I propose an innovation, a deviation from ALA-style cataloging practice, namely the principle of title main entry for all types of publications. This eliminates the traditional distinctions between author, title, and uniform title main entries with the attendant complications that make the ALA cataloging rules, and especially Chapter 21 of the Anglo-American Cataloguing Rules, difficult to understand.

Simplified small library cataloging, however, is logically in no way inferior to ALA-style library cataloging. All the concepts and practices introduced in this book, from the description principle to the layout of the catalog card and the fields of an on-line catalog database, are anchored in careful reasoning. Consequently, *Small Library Cataloging* may not be easy bedside reading. It requires close attention and a motivated reader. The reward for working through these chapters will be the good feeling that comes from knowing what one is doing. The study of this book will therefore simplify the reader's life in the library.

Credit for the idea of *Small Library Cataloging* belongs to Chuck Peterson of Santa Ana, California, custom bookbinder and friend to many people who run small libraries. The words, examples, and mistakes found in these pages, of course, remain the author's responsibility.

Introduction

In the beginning I picture your library as a room full of materials: hardbound and paperbound books, pamphlets, piles of magazine issues, a large dictionary, an encyclopedia, a few maps, a box full of audiotapes and compact discs, some color slides, and perhaps even a globe. All of it inherited from an earlier day, none of it cataloged, classified, or organized for use in any way. Let us say there are also some shelves, filing cabinets, a desk and chair, a typewriter, and such. But nothing else. Certainly no manual of procedures.

Or perhaps it is a fairly neat operation. Someone before you had it organized. There is a rudimentary card catalog, some of the books have labels on their spines with numbers typed on them, and several of the magazines have been bound.

Whatever shape your library is in as you take over, you will have at least two big questions: What is there to do? And what should be done first? There are three major tasks to be done, in this order:

1. Clean up and weeding
2. Organization and arrangement
3. Cataloging

CLEAN UP AND WEEDING

Clean up, here, does not mean dusting and scraping, although some of that may need to be done, too. What is meant in this context is the discarding of unwanted items. A good rule is to discard everything that is not relevant to the particular purposes your library is to serve. A hospital's medical library, for example, exists to provide medical information. It does not need a set of Reader's Digest condensed books, no matter how complete. A church library exists for the instruction and inspiration of clergy, church schoolteachers, and members of the congregation. It has no use for Taylor's *Introduction to Linear Algebra* or an old volume of the *United States Statutes at Large*. An elementary school library is intended to enhance the reading and discovery skills of ten-year-olds. It does not need Ernest Jones' *Life and Work of Sigmund Freud*, in three volumes. If you find such treasures but cannot bring yourself to throw the books away just yet, pack them in cardboard boxes and store them somewhere out of the way. There is nothing wrong with them, as such. They are merely irrelevant in the present context and will probably find a better home elsewhere. Maybe they can be offered to another library or sold at a book sale.

There is another class of irrelevant books that should be discarded: old books and old editions. A book entitled *So You Are Going to College: A Guide for Students*, dated 1923, is not likely to help today's young people prepare for their academic future. My advice: throw it away. Don't waste time and space cataloging such materials. Or take the sixth edition of *Introduction to Biochemistry*. The library has the ninth edition on the shelf, and the tenth is on order. My advice: throw the sixth edition away. It is probably a gift occasioned by someone else's housecleaning.

Duplicates, too, must be carefully evaluated. Sometimes they are needed. If a certain book is in constant demand, a gift copy would be most welcome. You may even buy a second copy. But more often than not one copy of a book is plenty. Duplicates must be justified for they take away space and absorb processing time. Very seldom should you accept a third copy of anything. If you are given four copies of a new book (new to the library, that is) that looks relevant, pick the two best-looking specimens and throw or give the others away.

Some of the things you find may be very relevant to your library but consist of incomplete sets—an encyclopedia without the index volume, for example, or perhaps a run of magazines from 1970 to 1990. It is a good idea to set aside such incomplete sets and hold on to them until everything else has been put in order. Sometimes missing volumes miraculously reappear, or two or three independent gifts combine to form a complete run of back issues of a desirable magazine.

Having discarded unwanted materials and set aside incomplete and doubtful ones, you are ready for the second task.

ORGANIZING

It is obvious that books, periodicals, cassettes, slides, and all other information media kept in the library must be put away according to some plan. That library is best in which things can be expected to be in certain places. The design of a good library organization plan presupposes a clear understanding of a number of principles derived primarily from the structural characteristics of the media stored in the library. It also requires a knowledge of the reasons and methods for grouping different kinds of library media apart from others and of the ways of arranging documents within their groups. Part I of this book, therefore, deals with questions of library organization in terms of the structure of publications, files of library materials, classification, shelf arrangement, and the marking of books. When that work is done and your books are on their shelves you are ready for the third task.

CATALOGING

For purposes of this book, cataloging means preparing bibliographic records and making them accessible to readers in an orderly arrangement so that the resulting index to the library's holdings is clear, consistent, and comprehensive.

Part II of this book is devoted to the logical principles that govern cataloging and to practical questions such as which description principle to apply, what to put into a bibliographic record, how to construct a main entry, what added entries to make, how to compose their headings, and what filing rules to use. Throughout this book it is assumed that readers are laypersons who will want to make their own cataloging decisions. Depending on where they find themselves, they may be helped by printed catalog cards available for some books, CIP (Cataloging-in-Publication), printed bibliographic aids, on-line aids, and other libraries' MARC (machine readable cataloging) records. Typically, they will type their own catalog cards.

Part III is intended to show how the computer can make library work easier by printing cards from a basic set of bibliographic data assembled by the lay cataloger, or by accumulating such bibliographic records to support an on-line catalog.

Part I

ARRANGEMENT OF PUBLICATIONS ON THE SHELF

Chapter One

Structure of Publications

Writing for laypeople in charge of small libraries, one is tempted to simplify things and begin by saying that library cataloging is the art of arranging books for use. This is a good statement, and it is true. But it does not say much. It does not even allow for the fact that, first of all, we must define what we mean by "books."

WHAT IS A BOOK?

Traditionally, books were sheets of paper bound together between covers, forming containers for someone's printed words. But today not all words that are recorded and stored as print on paper between covers, and not all those that are in print on paper are bound as books. Many words are recorded in spoken form on discs or on tape, or in printed form reduced to microfilm, or typed on single sheets and stapled. There are pamphlets, loose-leaf sets, periodicals, technical reports, films, videos, compact discs, and a variety of other media designed for the storage of information. Modern libraries house them all and keep them ready for use.

All of these information storage media can be said to be books in the general sense, while only some of them are print on paper books in the special sense. To remove the ambiguity from cataloging terminology, library textbooks and manuals nowadays avoid the term book altogether, speaking instead of items, documents, and works. But the terminology has not been standardized. To make it clear what we are discussing, we must carefully define these three terms.

First, a "work." The *ALA Glossary of Library and Information Science* (Chicago, American Library Association, 1983) states that a work is a defined body of recorded information, as distinct from the substance on which it is recorded. This definition can be expanded: a work is a unit of someone's intellectual, scholarly, or artistic creation. Examples of works, for our purposes here, are an essay, a story, a novel, a poem, a play, a theoretical treatise, an article, a paper, or a lecture.

The second term is "document." The *ALA Glossary* defines a document as a physical entity on or in which a work is recorded or on which several works or parts of works are recorded. As examples the glossary lists books and sound recordings, among other types. A document, then, is any physical storage unit, of any medium, that contains one or more works of recorded information.

To emphasize the distinction between a work and a document, we may want to consider a lecture. If it is published as print on paper it may appear as a book. But if it is published recorded on tape it may appear as a cassette. The book and the cassette are different documents. But the lecture is the same work in both cases.

The word "item," finally, has several meanings. In cataloging, the *ALA Glossary* states, item means bibliographic item. A bibliographic item is defined as a document or a set of documents treated as an entity and as such forming the basis for a single bibliographic description. In other words, an item can be either a single-document item or a multi-document item. Most novels (works) appear in books (documents) that are published as one physical volume (single-document item). But a large treatise may be one work published in two volumes. This would be a two-document item.

To make these distinctions clearer, here are some further examples. The book you are holding in your hand is an item, one bibliographic unit. It is also a document, one physical unit. And as it happens, it contains one sole work. This is the simplest kind of item there is. It can be described by a formula as follows:

1 ITEM, 1 DOCUMENT, 1 WORK

But not all items are that simply structured. On occasion a writer produces a work that, on publication, fills two books. The formula for such a work would be this:

1 ITEM, 2 DOCUMENTS, 1 WORK

Some publications contain many different works. A one-volume anthology, for example, may hold eighty poems. This would be the formula:

1 ITEM, 1 DOCUMENT, 80 WORKS

Or consider a set of compact discs that contain Beethoven's nine symphonies plus the Coriolan and the Prometheus overtures, eleven works all told on six discs. Here is the formula:

1 ITEM, 6 DOCUMENTS, 11 WORKS

Clearly, books or items, containers of recorded information, come in many different formats. But there is an underlying order to this world of publications. Given the definitions of work, document, and item shown above we can agree on the following formulation: all items cataloged in a library consist of one or more documents and contain one or more works.

And since the number of documents and works per item can vary and since items, documents, and works may or may not have individual titles, it seems that there are at least eight major structural types of items that all require slightly different treatment in cataloging. Table 1 will demonstrate these eight item types.

If all books were simple stand-alone works of type 1, each written by one author, the rules for classifying and cataloging books could be reduced to a one-page statement. But the structural diversity introduces an element of choice into the work of arranging books on the shelves. While some books come as single-volume items and can stand either here or there, others come in sets of two or more volumes. Some multivolume sets must stand together, while others can be treated either as sets in one location or as so many individual volumes dispersed in different locations.

Consider a two-volume set of books, an item consisting of two documents. Each volume contains a dozen essays by different authors. Volume 1 deals with American politics, volume 2 with European politics. If it is an item of type 4, the set might best be split up so that volume 1 can stand with all other books on American politics and volume 2 with all other books on European politics. But if it is an item of type 5, the set must stay together.

Table 1 Eight structural types of publications

			One work per docu-ment	More than one work per docu-ment	Multi-docu-ment item holds one work
Item consists of only one document			1	2	
Item consists of two or more documents	Closed item	Document titles as well as item title	3	4	
		Item title only		5	8
	Open item	Document titles as well as item title		6	
		Item title only		7	

From the point of view of the library user, the proper arrangement of books may spell the difference between finding and not finding required information. In fact, these decisions are crucial since the whole purpose of running a library is, of course, to facilitate the retrieval of stored information.

EXAMPLES

Here are a few schematics to exemplify different types of items. The first, shown in Figure 1, is a single-document item. It is an item consisting of one document. The entire contents of this item is one work. Since the book contains one work and stands alone, is not part of any set, one could call it a stand-alone work. It is a book of type 1. In such books the title of the item is also the title of the work contained in it. This is the most common type of book. It is easy to catalog, and library user looking for this work will have no trouble finding it in the catalog.

Figure 2 is an item that looks different but is also of type 1. This item also consists of one document that contains one work. The title of the disc is also the title of the work recorded on it. In terms of medium we distinguish between a tape, a cassette, an LP, or a compact disc on the one hand, and a book on the other hand, of course. But structurally there is no difference between them. The same cataloging principles apply, or should apply, to all items of type 1.

The book in Figure 3, too, stands alone. And it is an item of one document. But it contains essays or chapters by thirty-eight physicians, a total of sixty-three works. It is a book of type 2.

Urinary analysis and diagnosis
by Louis Heinzelmann.

Figure 1. Urinary Analysis and Diagnosis *by Louis Heinzelmann*

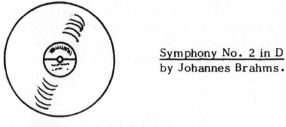

Symphony No. 2 in D
by Johannes Brahms.

Figure 2.   Symphony No. 2 in D *by Johannes Brahms*

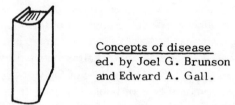

Concepts of disease
ed. by Joel G. Brunson
and Edward A. Gall.

Figure 3.   Concepts of Disease *edited by Joel
G. Brunson and Edward A. Gall*

As a document or item, this book is easy to catalog. But notice that the title of this item is not the title of any of the works in it. Each of the sixty-three works has its own title. The reader will appreciate the difficulties of a library user trying to locate one of these works unless the library has taken steps to provide access to these individual works by their authors, titles, and subject matter. But this takes us to the topic of analytics, dealt with in Chapter 10.

Figure 4 is an example of a multi-document item. These two volumes form the beginning of an open set of books, an annual series. Each book in the set contains numerous works. It is a set of type 7. This set must stay together in one location because the individual documents have no titles of their own. As in the previous example, extra steps would have to be taken if it were considered important to make the individual works available to library users.

Figure 5 is a closed set of two volumes that contains only one work. It is an item of type 8. Becker and Doe together wrote the whole book or, more precisely, the whole work which grew so large that it filled a set of two books. The entire set, of course, stands together in one loca-

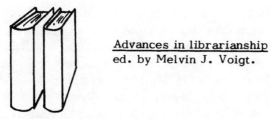

Advances in librarianship
ed. by Melvin J. Voigt.

Figure 4. Advances in Librarianship *edited by Melvin J. Voigt*

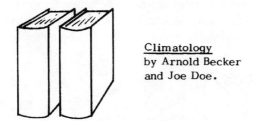

Climatology
by Arnold Becker
and Joe Doe.

Figure 5. Climatology *by Arnold Becker and Joe Doe*

tion and the work title is the same as the item title. It is an easy job to catalog and find this stand-alone work.

The two volumes in Figure 6 also form a closed set of two books, two documents. They contain contributions by a dozen writers, a total of fifteen works, each with its own distinctive work title. It is an item

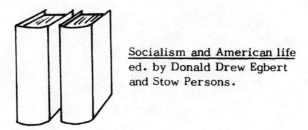

Socialism and American life
ed. by Donald Drew Egbert
and Stow Persons.

Figure 6. Socialism and American Life *edited by Donald Drew Egbert and Stow Persons*

of type 5. Since there are no individual document titles, the set stands together under its item title.

Sets of two or more volumes sometimes consist of individually titled documents. Figure 7 shows an example of an open set of type 6. Each of the numbered volumes in this item bears a different document title. Each of the books in the set deals with a different topic. Such a set may be broken up so that each book can be placed with others on its subject. But of course the set can also be left standing together, which requires a totally different classification and cataloging job.

These examples demonstrate the complexities of the structure of publications. Unless we clearly differentiate between an item, a document, and a work, we shall find it difficult to talk about organizing "books" in libraries, let alone about classifying and cataloging them.

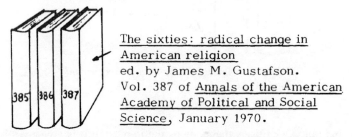

The sixties: radical change in American religion
ed. by James M. Gustafson.
Vol. 387 of Annals of the American Academy of Political and Social Science, January 1970.

Figure 7. The Sixties: Radical Change in American Religion *edited by James M. Gustafson; volume 387 of* Annals of the American Academy of Political and Social Science, *January 1970*

Chapter Two

Files, Shelf Arrangement, and Classification

FILE

A file, in the context of a library, is simply a location, a place for books and other publications. Some files consist of cabinets filled with manila folders. Some files are trays holding microfilm reels or fiches. Most library materials are housed on shelves. Thus, the entire stack area where the bulk of the books are kept is a file. If some shelves have been set aside for often-used reference books, these reference shelves are another file. It is not unusual even for small libraries to have a dozen different files.

Figure 8 shows the floor plan of a fictitious library where the materials are stored in six different files. To distinguish the files from each

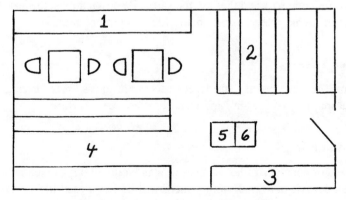

Figure 8. *Floor plan showing different files*

other they are given names. The six files in this hypothetical library have been named as follows: (1) Current periodicals; (2) Back issues; (3) Reference books; (4) Stacks; (5) Map case; and (6) Dictionary stand.

File Designations

Since the books that belong into the several files often have to be marked on the spines the corresponding catalog cards likewise have to be marked, and since the names of the files are somewhat long, abbreviated file designations are usually adopted. Thus, a file reserved for very large books may be called OVERSIZE, or perhaps FOLIO (a designation inherited from the printing industry of an earlier day), or simply "F." A file set aside for reference books is often designated by REF or perhaps "R." And so on. While the choice of a file designation is an arbitrary act, a few principles can be stated. First, the designation should, if possible, be self-explanatory. Thus, the designation REF or even R is better, and says more, than a green dot.

Second, the designation should be as small as is possible. A file used to store atlases and maps should not be designated GEOGRAPHICAL ATLASES AND MAPS. The short word ATLAS is better. One must remember that designations must fit on spine labels and catalog cards.

Third, the designation must not conflict with the notation of any classification system used. The file designation R for reference books should not be used if R is also the class symbol for medicine, as it is in many college libraries.

While there are probably not two libraries that are organized in exactly the same way and that use the same file designations, the arrangement of library materials into many files is common practice.

Open Files

Some files are directly and freely accessible to all library users. The great majority of files in American libraries are open files.

Closed Files

Closed or controlled files are files to which only library personnel have direct access. In a small library there will be few closed files. A possible example would be a file of slides arranged by a homemade system of codes that are meaningless to the library user. For efficient retrieval and to insure proper placement of returned slides the file might be restricted, to be serviced only by the librarian.

SHELF ARRANGEMENT

Fixed Location

Publications can be arranged within their files in many ways. In former times books were often arranged on shelves in a fixed location. A book marked 18/3, for example, was the third book from the left on shelf number 18. Fixed location shelving is not used much today, if at all, because it lacks hospitality, the ability to accommodate future insertions. When the shelf is full there is no way to insert a new book or a second copy between book 18/3 and book 18/4.

Accession Order

A modified fixed location order that is still used in many files today is the arrangement of publications on the shelves in the order of their arrival in the library. Each book is given an accession number as it is acquired and is filed by that number. The 117th book acquired will thus stand to the right of the 116th book. It will be followed by the 118th book, and so on, regardless of who wrote it and what it is about. This system, of course, has the same faults as the fixed location system: it disperses multiple copies of the same book, and different books on the same subject, more or less widely from each other.

Numerical Order

Some types of documents come equipped with a built-in system of numbers. For example, the California Division of Mines and Geology publishes at irregular intervals a series of "Special Reports" on different topics; these reports are numbered, beginning with SR 1 (1950). Another example is the Conference Board of New York, an independent business research organization; their periodically issued reports are numbered at the source and are cross-indexed by report numbers in an annual cumulative subject index. Serial publications of this type abound in many types of libraries. They are best kept together in one shelf section, arranged by their own numbers. This makes the librarian's work easier and it also guarantees easy retrieval.

Alphabetical Order

Some files, such as periodical back issues, can be kept in order alphabetically by title. An issue of *The Nation*, for example, can be clearly identified as such from the cover and placed between *Modern Age* and *Oceans*. If enough space is left between titles, alphabetical arrangement allows for the insertion of multiple copies and successive issues of the same title as well as for the addition of new titles. It is a relatively hospitable system for arranging publications that carry an easily visible name on the outside, such as magazines, maps, or certain pamphlet series. However, alphabetical order does not keep together publications that treat the same subject. Only classified arrangement will accomplish this.

CLASSIFICATION

By far the best known method of arranging books on library shelves is classification. Every American child is familiar with the decimal classification system, for example, which for many, under the name of "the Dewey system," has become a synonym for library classification in general.

The principle of book classification is simple enough: every book is assigned a relative position on the shelf according to a salient characteristic. This leads to the grouping of like publications within a file. There are many possible criteria for grouping. The best known is classification by subject.

Subject classification refers to the grouping of publications within a file according to their main subject. A certain medical book, for example, may contain one sole work about human anatomy and fit neatly into the class "Anatomy." Another book deals with human physiology and fits into the class "Physiology." When all like books are assigned consistently to these two classes, all books containing works on anatomy and all those on physiology will eventually stand together. This is the essence of subject classification.

But knowledge recorded in books and other types of publications is not restricted to such simple and clear-cut topics. In the field of mental health, for example, there is a class "Psychology" (BF in the Library of Congress classification system; 150 in the Dewey Decimal classification system) and a closely related class "Psychiatry" (RC 454 and 616.89, respectively). Since one book cannot stand both in 150 and in 616.89 a decision must be made. It takes expertise to do that properly. Consider a book such as James Covington Coleman's *Abnormal Psychology and Modern Life*. Since the title contains the word "psychology," a layperson might class this book in psychology. The expert, however, knows that it belongs with the books in psychiatry.

Also, many topics can be logically subdivided. In psychiatry we have books on neuroses and books on psychoses, for example. The books on psychoses may deal with functional psychoses or with organic psychoses. Books about functional psychoses may deal with schizophrenia or with paranoia, and so forth. The possible divisions are almost infinite and to determine authoritatively whether a given book such as *Betrayal of the Body*, by Alexander Lowen, should stand with other books on schizophrenia or with those on paranoia, or perhaps elsewhere, is no easy task.

It does not become easier if we consider that there are also collections of works. A certain book may hold, say, ten works, each about a certain well-defined topic. The book itself, being just the "empty container"— the term comes from a glossary published by the Educational Resources Information Center (ERIC)—has no subject at all. But each of the works in it has a different subject. To which subject area shall the item be assigned?

Nor does classification become easier if we add to these considerations the fact that works can deal with more than one topic simultaneously, either hierarchically related to a broader subject or not, as well as with several different relationships between topics, such as mental health and social class, mental health in a historical perspective, or mental health as an aspect of abnormal psychology.

Needless to say, the subtleties of subject classification often baffle even the experienced librarian. It is easy to find examples of inconsistency in the output of no lesser library than that of the United States Congress. In that library two unrelated books stand near to each other—*Social Statistics and the City* (HA29) and *Statistical*

Methods Applied to Experiments in Agriculture and Biology (HA 40)—while Beyer's *Handbook of Tables for Probability and Statistics* (QA276), closely related to the book on statistical methods in agriculture, stands far apart from it.

Clearly, the assignment of books to their proper places in a classification system is not a task for the unprepared. It seems naive to expect lay personnel placed in charge of small libraries to classify books as if there were nothing to it. Yet in practice that is exactly what usually happens. Administrators simply expect that the collection will be cataloged (often confusing "classification" with "cataloging"), and that will be that. A compromise solution to the dilemma must be found. Let us first discuss a few key terms.

Classes

Library classification systems are more or less carefully developed schedules of hierarchically related categories. They all attempt the same thing: to compartmentalize the complete body of knowledge within their scope in a logical fashion so that like books in the fields covered can be placed side by side on the shelves. A book thus compartmentalized is said to belong to a certain class.

Notations

Books and catalog cards must be marked so that they can be kept in order and retrieved. The names of classes are usually too long to fit in the available space on the spine of books and on catalog cards. It would be far too cumbersome to label a book, "Diseases of the cardiovascular system," which is one of the classes in the Dewey system. Instead, a so-called notation is introduced consisting of arbitrarily assigned short symbols that represent the long names of classes. In the Dewey system, the book on diseases of the cardiovascular system would belong to the class "616.1"; in the Library of Congress system it might belong to class "RC 669"; and in the system of the National Library of Medicine the proper notation would be "WG 100."

CLASSIFICATION SYSTEMS

Dewey Decimal Classification

The best known of the published classification systems is the decimal classification devised by Melvil Dewey 125 years ago. The Dewey system divides knowledge into ten arbitrarily established main classes presented in the following order:

0 Generalities
1 Philosophy
2 Religion
3 Social sciences
4 Language
5 Pure sciences
6 Technology
7 Arts
8 Literature
9 Geography and history

Each of the ten main classes is divided into ten "divisions." The main class "Religion," for example, is divided as follows:

20 Religion in general
21 Philosophy and theory of religion
22 Bible
23 Christianity, Christian theology
24 Christian moral and devotional theology
25 Local Christian churches and Christian religious orders
26 Christian social and ecclesiastical theology
27 Historical, geographic, persons treatment of Christianity
28 Denominations and sects of the Christian church
29 Comparative religion, religions other than Christianity

Note that a second digit was added to main class 2, Religion. It designates the division. Thus 22 means "main Class 2 Division 2," defined as "Bible." The resulting one hundred divisions are further subdivided into ten sections each. This means that a third digit is added to the main class and the division digits. The division "Bible," for example, is spread into ten sections as follows:

220   Bible in general
221   Old Testament
222   Historical books
223   Poetic books
224   Prophetic books
225   New Testament
226   Gospels and acts
227   Epistles
228   Revelation or Apocalypse
229   Apocryphal, etc.

Each of the sections is represented by a three-digit number. Thus, if we include "000," a total of 1,000 sections result.

Each section can be further subdivided as needed by adding decimals to the three-digit section number. In this way, for the long topic "Adaptation of animals to meteorological factors," a brief notation is substituted: 591.54. Catalogers refer to this kind of number as a "class" number or "Dewey" number.

In many cases it is possible to add decimal digits to base numbers according to seven mnemonic tables. Mnemonic (i.e., memorable, easy to remember) here means that the same combination of numbers always signifies the same attribute or characteristic. The table of standard subdivisions, for example, allows the combination of a subject base number like 591.54 with a standard subdivision like –09 for geographical or historical treatment. The resulting number, 591.5409, presumably stands for a book that treats geographically (or historically) the adaptation of animals to meteorological factors.

Another mnemonic table provides digits that stand for areas. Thus, –6 stands for Africa. Added to the standard subdivision –09, a number like this could result: 591.54096, for "adaptation of African animals to meteorological factors."

Although biography can hardly be called an "area," one area division, –2, is nevertheless very useful. If added to the standard subdivision –09 it makes a handy device for collecting all biographies in a subject class together. Thus, if theology carries the Dewey number 230, then biographies of theologians are in 230.92.

The entire classification system, now in the 21st edition, is available for purchase from OCLC Forest Press, 6565 Frantz Rd, Dublin, OH 43017–3300 (614–764–6000). The system is used in thousands of general libraries in America.

Abridged Dewey Classification

There is an abridged version of the decimal system, also designed for general libraries (libraries that cover all subjects from philosophy to science and art). The abridged version provides fewer but broader classes with shorter notations. A book dealing with animal adaptation to meteorological factors would be placed into the subsection 591.5 (animal ecology).

Paradoxical as it sounds, for a small special collection concentrating on detailed aspects of a narrow subject area the abridged version is less suitable than the full Dewey classification because it results in all books falling into a few broad classes. In a technical library dealing with the desulfuration, storage, mechanical treatment, and physical properties of coal, for example, all books would stand in the same subsection 662.6 for "Coal." In many cases, then, using the abridged Dewey classification would be equivalent to no classification at all.

Applying the Decimal Classification

The Dewey tables are not completely logical. Like all other classification systems, the Dewey system must struggle with interrelationships of knowledge that are so complex that it may not be possible to maintain a clearly logical system.

A book on the theory of corporate financial reporting (655.3) stands right next to a completely unrelated directory of book and periodical publishers (655.4). The literature of Romance languages goes into 879.9, but the literature of one Romance language, Catalan, is placed elsewhere, in 849.9. The number for the whole of the Old Testament (221) is on the same level as the number for the historical books of the Bible (222), but those books, being a subdivision of the Old Testament, should logically be subdivisions of 221.

Time divisions and topical divisions of a subject are often in conflict. Thus there is a section 723 for medieval architecture (a time division) and a section 726 for church buildings (a topical division). There is no convenient slot for medieval churches.

The extensive analytical index presents hundreds of alphabetized, and therefore logically unrelated, terms in a terse, telescopic style. The index might list specific subtopics under a broader topic, but gives no hint how to find a number for a book that deals with the broad topic in general.

Public opinion notwithstanding, the use of the Dewey classification is not simple but quite difficult. No shortcuts can be offered here. However, over the years many books have been written on the application of the Dewey system and related subjects. Two publishing firms that are particularly active in this area are Libraries Unlimited, Box 6633, Englewood, CO 80155–6633 (800–237–6124), and H. W. Wilson Co., 950 University Av., Bronx, NY 10452–4224 (800–367–6770).

Library of Congress Classification

The Library of Congress system is a widely used general classification system that in the print version fills some thirty-odd volumes. The notation is alphanumeric (i.e., includes both letters and numbers) and irregular: some classes use single letters (E, F), some two (HX, LB), some three (KFC). Finer breakdowns are numerical, some using integers (HX1, F700), some decimal fractions (KFC 30.5, LB 1028.5).

The Library of Congress system is uneven in its treatment of subjects, often inconsistent, and its notation is not hierarchical in structure. Although it offers more separate main classes than the Dewey system, it is harder to use because it lacks a comprehensive index. Consequently, even catalogers in large and prestigious libraries find it difficult to be consistent. Consider these two books for example: *Composition of Scientific Words*, by R. W. Brown, and *The Scientist's Thesaurus*, by G. F. Steffanides. Both serve the same purposes and are almost identical in layout. Yet in spite of these obvious similarities the Library of Congress placed one in class PE1175, the other in class Q179.

Other Subject Classifications

Many special classification schemes have been published. The National Library of Medicine, for example, has developed a well-known system for medical books. Harvard University has developed a classification for business literature. The American Mathematical Society has published a classification scheme for the field of mathematics. The Art Libraries Society of North America has published an art classification. Volunteers or appointees in charge of small special libraries will probably do best to adopt one of the published classification schemes designed for their type of library. Help and advice can be had from the Cataloging and Classification Section of the Association for Library Collections & Technical Services, a division of the American Library Association, 50 East Huron Street, Chicago, IL 60611 (www.ala.org).

Help can also be had from the Special Libraries Association, 1700 Eighteenth Street, N. W., Washington, DC 20009 (www.sla.org). The addresses of numerous other American and Canadian library associations can be found in a useful directory entitled *Bowker Annual of Library and Book Trade Information*, available from the R. R. Bowker Co. in New Providence, NJ.

Form Classification

Subject arrangement is not the only alternative for the organization of library materials. Some types of books are best grouped on the shelves by their form rather than by their subject. A collection of stories about railways, for example, might stand with other collections of the genre "stories," not with other books about railways. The plays of Shakespeare, although they might deal with English history, do not stand with other books about English history. Nor do they stand with books about English literature. They *are* English literature and stand with all other books by Shakespeare.

Often subject and form principles are combined. A publication may be classed first by subject (for example, political science) and then by form (for example, periodical). The effect will be to separate political science materials that are periodicals from those that are not periodicals.

In some classes a book may be arranged first by language, then by genre, followed by time period, and finally subarranged by author. In such a classification books of like genre stand together, such as all German poetry. But it is also possible to group the books first by time period, then by author, and last by genre. Now all books by an author stand together, regardless of genre, perhaps all the plays, poems, essays, and stories by Bertolt Brecht. Many other variations are possible, all of which helps to explain why classification is a difficult art.

Constructing Your Own Classification System

Should it be necessary to construct an original classification scheme—not recommended but unavoidable under certain pressures of real life—the following guidelines are offered:

1. There should be a separate class for every subject field in which 25 to 50 books can be expected to fall. A small library (under 5,000 volumes) should not need more than 200 subject classes.
2. The classes should be mutually exclusive. These two classes are mutually exclusive: dogs, cats. They are mutually exclusive in the sense that a cat cannot also be a dog. The following two classes are not mutually exclusive: dogs, poodles. They are not mutually exclusive because a poodle is also a dog. It may be necessary in some cases to have a hierarchical class structure showing genus-species relationships. Ideally this should be handled by a class/subclass structure, e.g., Class DOGS, Subclass 1 POODLES, Subclass 2 TERRIERS, etc.
3. In addition to subject classes there should be a number of form classes, so called because they are places where books can be grouped together that share a certain format rather than a subject. Here are some suggested form classes:
   - Atlases (collections of geographical maps)
   - Bibliographies (lists of books, periodical indexes)
   - Biographical directories (e.g., *Who's Who*)
   - Dictionaries (books that define terminology)
   - Directories (lists of firms, suppliers)
   - Encyclopedias and handbooks
   - Tables of numerical values
4. There should be a general or miscellaneous class. Any book that does not fit into one of the established form classes will be placed into its subject class. If it does not fit in any subject class either, it will go into the general class until a better place for it is found. Accumulations in the general or miscellaneous class will soon show what additional classes are needed in the system.
5. Short notations, no more than three or four symbols per line, should be adopted.

STEP-BY-STEP GUIDE TO CLASSIFYING

The work of classifying a book is in several steps. I suggest that the reader go over the following questions once or twice, then apply the steps to individual books that come up for classifying:

Step 1. Is it a book about something (about the weather, for example, or about George Washington), or is it a book of a certain kind (a novel, for example, or a Spanish-English dictionary)?

Step 2. If it is a book about something, is the entire book about the same thing or does it deal with several subjects?

Step 3. If it deals with one subject, name that subject. Match that name with the narrowest of the established classes that will fit and assign the corresponding notation to the book.

Step 4. If it deals with several subjects, can these subjects all be said to be sub-topics of one broader topic? If so, name the broader topic and match that name with the best-fitting of the established classes. Assign the corresponding notation to the book.

Step 5. If it deals with several subjects that cannot be said to be sub-topics of one broader topic, name the topic that is either most thoroughly covered or of predominant interest to the type of user for whom the library exists. Match that name with the best fitting of the established classes. Assign the corresponding notation to the book.

Step 6. If it is not a book about something so much as a book of a certain format, name that format (dictionary? encyclopedia? almanac? handbook? collection of tables? bibliography?) and match that name with the best-fitting of the established classes. Assign the corresponding notation to the book.

Step 7. If it is not a book about something so much as a book containing a work or works of a certain genre, name that genre (novel? poems? plays? children's fairy tales?). Match that name with the best fitting of the established classes. Assign the corresponding notation to the book.

Bibliographic listings such as the *American Book Publishing Record* regularly include Dewey and Library of Congress class numbers for new books. On-line library catalogs available on the Internet also reveal how other libraries have classified a book. This often helps classifiers check on their own work and refine their understanding of the system and the classifying process. However, just because someone else assigned a book to a certain class does not guarantee that the result represents the best decision for your library. In a certain issue of the *American Book Publishing Record*, for example, two books about survey sampling were listed. One had been classed in Library of Congress QA276.6, the other in HA31.2, which shows again that it is not easy to keep like things together in a library. To decide what constitutes "like things" remains a highly subjective business.

Chapter Three

Location Codes or "Call Numbers"

Books and other types of items are often kept in order on their shelves by means of symbols that together constitute a location code. Many librarians, remembering the days when such codes were simple numbers and one had to call for one's books at a counter after looking them up in the catalog, still refer to the location code or parts of it as the "call number." A location code or call number may consist of as many as four parts:

1. File designation
2. Class symbol
3. Book symbol
4. Copy symbol

FILE DESIGNATIONS

The person who returns publications to their positions in the file must be able to tell, of course, into which file they belong. This is easy to do in the case of some kinds of publications. Current periodical issues, for example, are clearly recognizable as such by their format and name. A book (in the traditional sense) is identified by its shape and size as a publication that belongs in the book stacks.

Such publications do not need a special file designation. It is obvious in which file they belong. But for a current periodical issue to be distinguishable from a back issue, for example, or an ordinary book from one relegated to the reference file, the publications must carry visible file designations.

Designations for special files are arbitrary symbols, of course. The designation for certain reference books may be REF. Recordings such as compact discs may be housed in a file designated CD or MUSIC, and so on. All file designations have two purposes in common: they serve to tell library personnel into which file any given publication needs to be put, and they tell the catalog user in which file a given publication can be found.

In most libraries the bulk of the books belongs to one general collection often referred to as "the stacks." This file needs no designation. The file designation for such a book, we might say, is implied. In other words, if the location code mentions no other file, and if the publication is not clearly placed into a special file due to its format (e.g., a compact disc), the book belongs in the stacks. Here is an example of a location code with an "implied" file designation:

811.52
B7
W5

Absence of a special file designation in this location code means that the book belongs in the general file, "the stacks." This particular location code, by the way, was assigned to a book entitled *What the Woman Lived: Selected Letters of Louise Brogan*. By contrast, here is the location code for a book entitled *Historical Atlas of California*. It resides in a specially designed piece of furniture called an atlas case, and it carries a special file designation:

ATLAS
CASE
911.784
B4

The file designation here is ATLAS CASE.

CLASS SYMBOLS

The second part of the location code is the class symbol. If the decimal classification is used, the class symbol for a certain book of short stories may be

813.54

If the Library of Congress system is used, the symbol may be

PZ4

or possibly

PS 3562 .E42

Some class symbols in the Dewey system are very long. A certain book on the history of mountaineering, for example, was given this number:

796.52094947

Even bigger numbers are possible. Class symbols in the Library of Congress system, too, can get unwieldy. A book on nursing in the State of Oaxaca, Mexico, for example, might carry this class symbol:

RT
7
M6
O2

Here RT 7 stands for nursing, M6 stands for Mexico, and O2 stands for Oaxaca. All of that is one class symbol. If the library has several books on this topic, they all have the same class symbol. To distinguish them from one another, book symbols must be added to the location code.

BOOK SYMBOLS

File designations and class symbols alone do not contain all the information needed for a book to be found or replaced on the shelf. Suppose you were using the classification system of the National Library of Medicine and you had placed three books on hygiene in class QT275. There is nothing in that class number that would place these three books on the shelf in any particular relationship to each other. The three books could stand in any order as shown in Figure 9.

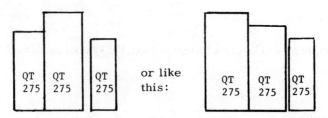

Figure 9. *Call numbers without book symbols*

They are not uniquely identified, and while many libraries use non-specific call numbers such lack of precision is generally not desirable. Ideally, every book should have its definite place on the shelf. This is why libraries often add book symbols to class symbols in order to compose a location code that is unique. The book symbol, as its name indicates, identifies the particular book. It is a symbol derived either from the title or from the author's name.

Suppose the three books on hygiene, referred to above, were entitled *Modern Health, You and Your Body*, and *How to Take Care of Yourself*, respectively. Their location codes, consisting of class symbol and book symbol, might be as follows:

	QT	QT	QT
class symbol	275	275	275
book symbol	H7	M7	Y7

The book symbols H7, M7, and Y7 are merely short notations for the first words in the titles, in alphabetical order:

How H7
Modern M7
You Y7

There are several ways to construct book symbols. Some libraries rely on the so-called Cutter Tables, a published system of fixed symbols assigned to certain letter combinations such as

Bilby B 491
Bile B 492
Bill B 493

The Cutter system has the virtue of consistency. It generates definite symbols for each combination of letters. The other side of that coin, of course, is a certain lack of flexibility. If a book entitled *Bill before the House* carries the book symbols B493, a later acquisition in the same class entitled *Bill before Law* must be given an arbitrary number interpolated between Bile and Bill, perhaps B4925.

A slightly more flexible system is the author number system pioneered by the Library of Congress. Here, specific letter combinations do not have fixed numbers. Instead, book symbols are constructed afresh in each subject class according to a formula. If the book number is based on the letter B, for example, the Library of Congress' system gives this direction:

... for second letter:	a	e	i	o	r	u
use number:	3	4	5	6	7	8

Under this system, *Bill before the House* in class X might be assigned the symbols B5; *Bill before Law*, if in another class such as Y, might get the same symbols, B5. But if both books were in class X, then the second book might get the symbol B4. Or, if B4 had already been used, B45 or some other number interpolated to preserve the alphabetical order. The complete system of book numbers, actually designated "author" numbers by the Library of Congress, was first published on pages 7 and 8 of the *Cataloging Service Bulletin*, Number 107 for December 1973, published by the Processing Department of the Library of Congress.

Book numbers preserve alphabetical order, incidentally, because they are treated as decimals. Thus the sequence B4, B45, B4952, B5 is treated as if the numbers were written 0.4, 0.45, 0.4952, and 0.5. This "implied decimals" stratagem applies to Cutter numbers as well as to Library of Congress author numbers.

Some small libraries assign abbreviated book symbols. A book on cancer entitled *Treatment of Cancer* and one entitled *Treatment of Carcinoma* might both have the same location code:

616.9   616.9
T   T

This diminishes the effectiveness of the location code. If both are on the shelf a reader must now investigate which of the two books he wants. If only one is on the shelf the reader may inadvertently take home the wrong book. It is better to establish unique book symbols based on a difference in the wording of the titles so that different books are clearly distinguishable:

616.9	616.9
T6	T7
. . . cancer	. . . carcinoma

Similar advice applies to books that differ in terms of their editions. The 6th edition (1986) of a certain book may bear the location code

R
121
K5

The library now acquires the 7th edition (1993) of the same book. The two editions rest side by side on the shelf. The year of the later edition can be added to its location code so that the books are clearly distinguished:

R
121
K5
1993

Since the book symbols as recommended here are based on the title of the book, it will happen that books by a given author are widely dispersed within a class. If it is desirable to keep books in a class together by their authors, as for example in a collection of literature, and the classification system used does not collect them in one place, the book symbol can be constructed on the basis of the author's name. This, of course, is why the book symbols of the Library of Congress are referred to as "author" numbers.

One idea behind author numbers is "collocation," a technical term that means that all of an author's works in a class stand in one place. It should be pointed out that collocation by means of author numbers is an illusion. It cannot be done reliably. If all the works of an author were free standing, separately cataloged units written by that author alone, collocation would indeed be possible. But many works are cooperative efforts of several authors, and many more are embedded with other authors' works in anthologies. Book numbers for such publications will have to be based on other criteria, such as title, and this spoils the idea of collocation. Nevertheless, here are the book numbers for the three hygiene books discussed above. We assume that their authors' names had been Able, Baker, and Chomsky, respectively:

QT   QT   QT
275 275 275
A2   B2   C5

Here is another example. Two stand-alone works by George Robert Gissing, *Nether World* and *Thyrza*, are classed in Dewey 823.8. The location codes may look as follows:

823.8   823.8
G45   G45
N3   T5

The book symbols here have been expanded and consist of an author component (G45) and a title component (N3 and T5, respectively).

Other expansions of the book symbol are possible. If *Nether World* were also available in a Spanish translation by Moreno, it might bear this location code:

823.8   (class)
G45   (author)
N3   (title)
M7   (translator)

Here is another possible treatment of the same book:

823.8
G15
N3m

where the "m" stands for the translator's name. Here is still another possibility:

823.8   (class)
G15   (author)
N3   (title)
Sp   (language)

When a corporate agency can be considered to be the author of the work or works in the item cataloged, the name of that agency can be used to form the book number. In this way all the law codes in a corporate library, for example, could be made to stand together by state, as in this example:

348   348   . . .348
C2   C2   . . .T3
M7   P3   . . .H2

where C2 stands for California, T3 for Texas.

When two or more copies of the same book are in the collection, a copy symbol is often added to the location code, beginning with copy 2. Suppose a book designated by the location code QT275 A2 is very popular and you have a total of three copies in the library. They might be labeled as follows:

QT   QT   QT
275   275   275
A2   A2   A2
c.2   c.3

The location code appears on the spine of the book and, if pockets and cards are used for lending, on the pocket and book card. Some libraries repeat the entire location code somewhere inside the book in case the label should fall off.

There was a time when location codes were hand-lettered onto spines in white or black ink. Nowadays most libraries type the code onto labels that are glued to spines, pockets, and cards. To prevent spine labels from peeling off, many libraries reinforce them with transparent tape that can be bought for the purpose from library supply houses. Others simply coat them generously with transparent glue before shelving the books.

SUMMARY OF STEPS FOR LOCATION CODES

1. Does the publication require a location code? Not all publications require them. Magazines, for example, often are kept on the shelves in alphabetical order by title.
2. If the publication does require a location code, does the publication belong to a special file that needs to be singled out? If so, assign a file designation.
3. Does the publication belong to a file that is arranged by accession numbers? If so, add the accession number to the file designation.
4. Does the publication belong to a classified file? Classify and assign the class symbol (notation).
5. Assign the book symbol from the title. Or, if the contents are all by one author, you may base the book symbol on the author's name.
6. Is this a second or subsequent copy of the same publication for this library? If so, add copy symbol to location code, but only on spine label, pocket, and book card, not on the catalog cards.

Part II

CATALOGING

Chapter Four

Description Principle

It is not enough to place publications onto the shelves of a library. To retrieve the information contained in them a catalog must be provided, an index to the library's collection that will enable the reader to look up a clue such as an author's name, a title, or a topic, and determine if the library has the book or books sought, and if so, where they are located. The books, in other words, have to be cataloged.

On one level, cataloging is the art of describing and indexing bibliographic items that contain recorded information. An item is described by writing down or otherwise recording its title, its author(s) or editor(s), its publisher, place and date of publication, and similar descriptive information.

On a deeper level, cataloging also involves the description and indexing of the works contained in multi-work items. But this is a topic we shall consider later.

Before an item can be described, however, the cataloger must consider two different description principles and decide which one to apply. When a publication is a single physical document this decision is easy: obviously, the document in hand—the book, the compact disc, the cassette, or whatever—is the item that the cataloger must describe. We can say that the document description principle applies.

But when a publication consists of more than one document per item, such as a set of three separate books that belong together, a choice may have to be made: the set as a whole may have a title and one description might cover the entire set. We can then say that the set description principle is applied. However, it is also possible that each book in the set has its own title. In that case the set could be split up and its component documents cataloged as separate units. We would say that the document description principle is applied. Whether such a set will be split up in a given library is a question of policy based on utility.

DOCUMENT DESCRIPTION PRINCIPLE

An example for the document description principle is the book entitled *Urinary Analysis and Diagnosis*, 5th edition, by Louis Heinzelmann, shown in Chapter 1 (Figure 1). It is a one-volume item and can only be described under the document description principle in terms of the title and author. Two other examples shown in Chapter 1 are the recording *Symphony No. 2 in D*, by Johannes Brahms (Figure 2), and the book *Concepts of Disease*, edited by Joel G. Brunson (Figure 3). Both publications stand alone, and are thus described under the document description principle.

SET DESCRIPTION PRINCIPLE

An example for the set description principle is the multi-volume set *Advances in Librarianship*, edited by Melvin J. Voigt, shown in Chapter 1 (Figure 4). Since the individual volumes in this set have no titles of their own the set must stay together. It is therefore described under the set description principle in terms of the set title and editor. A similar example, also shown in Chapter 1, is the two-volume set *Climatology*, by Arnold Becker and Joe Doe (Figure 5). This set contains one large work that fills two books. Of course the two volumes must also stay together. These two examples require no decision. There is only one possible way to describe them. But sometimes there is a choice.

DECISION: DOCUMENT OR SET?

Another set shown in Chapter 1 is entitled *The Sixties: Radical Change in American Religion*, ed. by James M. Gustafson, being v. 387 of the *Annals of the American Academy of Political and Social Science*, January 1970 (Figure 7). Each volume of the *Annals* has its own title and deals with a different subject. It would therefore be quite logical to treat each volume as a separate book under the document description principle, making separate catalog cards for each volume. If such a set is more useful standing together, however, it can be cataloged as one item under the set description principle (just one set of catalog cards for the entire set).

The following list of options may help catalogers to decide which description principle to apply. We refer to the table of eight publication types given in Chapter 1 (Table 1).

1. If the item cataloged is of types 1 or 2, the document description principle applies without exception.
2. If the item cataloged is of types 5, 7, or 8, the set description principle applies without exception.
3. If the item to be cataloged is of types 3, 4, or 6, it is usually kept together, i.e., the set description principle is applied. But the set can also be taken apart and treated as so many separate books, i.e., the document description principle can be applied if a purpose is served thereby. In either case it may be necessary to make some relational entries, a procedure that is discussed in Chapter 10.

Chapter Five

Preparing Catalog Cards: The Main Entry

Once the description principle for the publication to be cataloged has been decided upon the actual cataloging, i.e., the creation of entries, can begin. By the term "entry" we mean one catalog record. For the great majority of items it is correct to say that an entry is the same thing as a catalog card. But sometimes the catalog record is so extended (long title, several authors, etc.) that it takes two or more cards to hold all the information. In such a case the entire decklet of cards constitutes one entry.

It should be noted that not all librarians agree with this terminology. Some use the term "entry" to designate the heading that appears across the top of a card. In this book the term "entry" always means "one catalog record" or, in terms taken from the *Anglo-American Cataloguing Rules*, "a record of an item in a catalogue," while a "heading" is "a name, word, or phrase placed at the head of a catalogue entry."

In these pages the term "main entry," in accordance with the terminology of the *ALA Glossary*, is defined as the "complete catalog record of a bibliographic item." For each item cataloged we must make a main entry. If needed we can make added entries. An added entry record, like a main entry record, is also a catalog record of a bibliographic item. But it is not necessarily as complete as the main entry record, and in addition it carries an added entry heading across the top. These headings give access by authors' names, subjects, forms, or titles, as needed. That is why headings are often referred to as "access points." A discussion of added entry records and their headings begins with Chapter 7. In Chapters 5 and 6 we are concerned only with the main entry.

What information is needed for a complete catalog record? And how shall this information be arranged on the catalog card? Opinions are divided. Some librarians distinguish between author main entries (complete catalog records that carry the name of one author as a heading at the top), uniform title main entries (complete catalog records that carry a uniform title as a heading at the top), and plain title main entries (complete catalog records that have no headings but begin with the title). A distinction is also made between closed entries and open entries. Each type of main entry is constructed to slightly different specifications spelled out in a code that is followed widely, the *Anglo-American Cataloguing Rules* (AACR2).

To decide which type of main entry to make from case to case requires mastery of chapter 21 of AACR2, a complex 70-page treatise in itself. The rules are so involved and convoluted that they are sometimes hard to understand. That is why for years the Library of Congress has been publishing its own "rule interpretations." Obviously, small libraries often do not have personnel specially trained to cope with esoteric knowledge such as, for example, the difference between an "original author considered responsible" (Rule 21.12A) and an "original author no longer considered responsible" (Rule 21.12B), or perhaps determining if the work at hand is "a work that consists of a text for which an artist has provided illustrations" (Rule 21.11A1) or "a work of collaboration between a writer and an artist" (Rule 21.24A). This is why, rather than allow the cataloging operation to bog down in a maze of seemingly unmanageable complications, I propose a simplification of this process. For small libraries I recommend that all main entries be constructed as title main entries. By this stratagem one rule will apply to all publications. No exceptions.

A title main entry record for an item consists of five elements of bibliographic information:

1. Bibliographic description, starting with the title
2. The physical description of the item
3. Notes
4. Tracings, a record of all added entries made
5. Location code, sometimes designated the "call number"

Just what data make up these elements will be explained in Chapter 6. Here we are concerned only with the general form of the main entry record.

TITLE MAIN ENTRY LAYOUT

Figure 10 is a title main entry card. The example we selected comes from the Library of Congress. It was constructed in accordance with AACR2. It is a closed entry, which means that it is for a book that was complete when published.

For almost a hundred years the Library of Congress used to sell ready-made cards like these, which was a great help for small libraries. But that service was discontinued in 1997. When cards are typed locally the layout can be simplified, but it is best to follow one set of typographic specifications throughout so that all cards have the same indentions. One possible card layout is illustrated in Figure 11.

The indentions, or spaced margins, shown here (2, 12, and 14 spaces from the left edge of the card) are quite arbitrary. Any other convenient combination will do just as well.

The reader should notice that the topmost paragraph or block, labeled "bibliographic description," is always typed indented to the left, or in

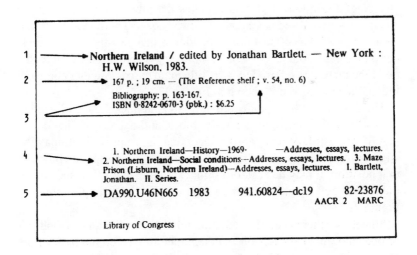

Legend: 1. Bibliographic description; 2.
Physical description; 3. Notes; 4. Tracings ;
5. Call number.

Figure 10. *Printed Library of Congress catalog card*

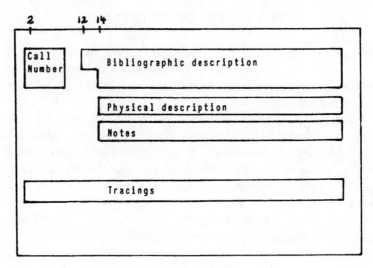

Figure 11. *Schematic showing indentions*

"hanging" indention. It always contains the bibliographic description which, as we shall see in Chapter 6, always begins with the title of the item cataloged. The effect of the indention is that the title always stands out on the card. And since such a main entry record begins with the title of the item, it is referred to as a "title main entry." Another complete title main entry record is shown in Figure 12.

The reader will have noticed that in all examples the location code or "call number" occupies a special block in the upper left hand corner of the card. When word processing is employed, it may be slightly inconvenient or inefficient to program for a separate block in that position. It may be easier to print cards line by line. In such cases the location code can be given as a note, as in the example shown in Figure 13.

Sometimes there is more cataloging information than fits on the front of one card. In such cases one can continue to type on the back of the card (upside down and hole at the top for easier reading when the card is held in the tray by the rod) or one can make one or more extension cards for the entry. Figure 14 shows an example of an entry that consists of a card and an extension card.

```
BF
441        Identifying and solving problems : a
K27        system approach / Roger Kaufman. --
           La Jolla, CA : University Associates,
           1976.
           iv, 121 p. : ill. ; 16 x 23 cm.




1. PROBLEM SOLVING.   I. Kaufman, Roger A.
```

Figure 12. *A title main entry card*

```
        Larousse encyclopedia of European
        history / General editor: Joseph
        Hyslop. -- New York : Klamm, 1945.
        508 p.

        LOCATION: 909 L2




1. EUROPE--HISTORY.   I. Hyslop, Joseph, ed.
```

Figure 13. *An example showing call number in center of card*

```
F            History of Los Angeles County,
868             California, with illustrations,
L8              descriptions of its scenery,
R7              residences, fine blocks and
                manufactories, from original
                sketches by artists of the
                highest ability / edited by
                William Willoughby Robinson
                and Clara Pintel Diamond.
                Berkeley, CA : Howell, 1948.
     (continued on next card)
```

```
F            History of Los Angeles County,
868                                  card 2 of 2
L8
R7              192 p.
                Reproduction of the Thompson
                edition of 1885.




     1. LOS ANGELES (COUNTY), CALIFORNIA.
     I. Robinson, William Willoughby, ed.
```

Figure 14. *An extension card*

OTHER TYPES OF MAIN ENTRIES

Author Main Entries

It should be noted again that the simplified title main entry concept introduced in the present book is more practical, but it is not the standard according to the instructions of AACR2. Most "standard" main entries are author main entry records, which means that they have an author heading above the bibliographic description. The idea of constructing a main entry record with an author heading on top derives from the correct observation that many items are stand-alone works by one author or collections of several works by one author. In such cases it is quite logical to consider the author's name the most important element of the bibliographic description and to construct a main entry record in such a way that the author's name stands at the head, above the title, last name first for easy filing.

Figure 15 shows an example of an author main entry. It begins with the name of the author in a separate paragraph or block at the top of the card, "Kaufman, Roger A." This is the main entry heading. The paragraph below the heading, beginning with the word "Identifying" and ending with "1976," is the bibliographic description, complete with author's name in regular form, first name first.

Many items are issued under the sponsorship of a corporate agency rather than by an author in the usual sense. Under certain circumstances this calls for a so-called corporate author main entry, a main entry record that carries the name of a corporate body as a heading above the bibliographic description. An example of a corporate author main entry is the Library of Congress card shown in Figure 16.

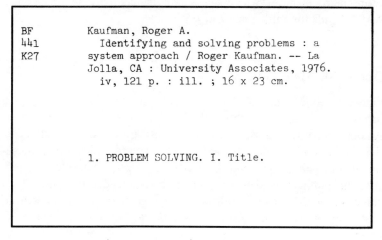

```
BF        Kaufman, Roger A.
441          Identifying and solving problems : a
K27       system approach / Roger Kaufman. -- La
          Jolla, CA : University Associates, 1976.
             iv, 121 p. : ill. ; 16 x 23 cm.




          1. PROBLEM SOLVING. I. Title.
```

Figure 15. *An author main entry card*

Main entry

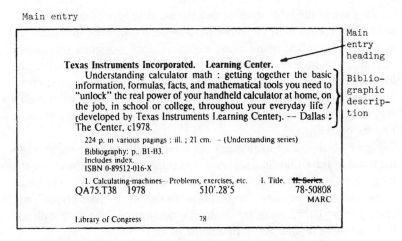

Figure 16. *A Library of Congress corporate author main entry*

Unfortunately, the principle of making a main entry under an author heading is often very difficult to carry out because determining authorship is by no means always a simple matter. While all works, of course, have been written or created by persons, or authors, the names of these persons are not always known. Some items contain many works by different authors and no one author can be said to be responsible for the entire item. In cases where the author cannot be determined even AACR2 calls for a title main entry.

Open Title Main Entries

Figure 17 shows an open title main entry for the *Tanner Lectures*, a series of books that are published year after year in separate volumes. An open entry, of course, has no final publication date. Instead, it carries the beginning date followed by a hyphen to indicate that the series is still being published. By tradition, if not for any logical reason, the publication date in open entries precedes the publisher's name, in closed entries it follows the name. A small library will do best to ignore such fine distinctions and place the date always in the same place.

Main entry

```
BD                                                          Biblio-
232        The Tanner lectures on human values.      ⎞     graphic
T3            vol. 1 -          1982 -               ⎟      descrip-
           Salt Lake City, UT : University of Utah   ⎬     tion
           Press ; Cambridge : Cambridge University  ⎟
           Press.                                    ⎠
              v. ; 24 cm.


           1. VALUES--ADDRESSES, ESSAYS, LECTURES.
```

Figure 17. *An open entry*

Uniform Title Main Entries

Some publications are best kept together under an artificial collective title, a so-called uniform title. In some cases, AACR2 calls for a uniform
title main entry like the one shown in Figure 18.

Main entry

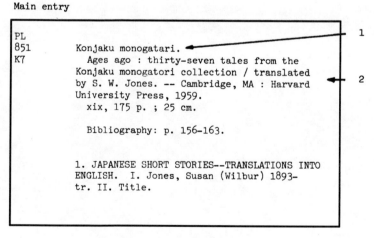

```
PL                                                          1
851        Konjaku monogatari. ◄
K7            Ages ago : thirty-seven tales from the
           Konjaku monogatori collection / translated
           by S. W. Jones. -- Cambridge, MA : Harvard  ◄   2
           University Press, 1959.
              xix, 175 p. ; 25 cm.

           Bibliography: p. 156-163.


           1. JAPANESE SHORT STORIES--TRANSLATIONS INTO
           ENGLISH.  I. Jones, Susan (Wilbur) 1893-
           tr. II. Title.
```

Figure 18. *A uniform title main entry*

When the title main entry principle, as recommended in these pages, is adopted for the bulk of the library's books there is, of course, little need to construct author or uniform title main entries. More about the how of title main entries is given in Chapter 6.

Chapter Six

What Goes on the Title Main Entry

The previous chapter stated that the title main entry record consists of five elements: (1) the bibliographic description, (2) the physical description, (3) notes, (4) tracings, and (5) location code. These elements need to be discussed in detail.

THE BIBLIOGRAPHIC DESCRIPTION

The bibliographic description typically consists of the title, statement of authorship, edition statement, and imprint.

Title

This first element is always present in any bibliographic record. If the item does not have a title, the cataloger must give it one. There can be no exceptions because the title is the one element without which a publication cannot be described. A catalog card without a title would be an incomplete catalog record. As far as the bibliographic description is concerned, therefore, all publications have a title, a name given to them either by their creators or by some later bibliographer. A note concerning terminology: to distinguish between titles found on title pages and titles supplied by librarians, I have called them natural titles and uniform titles, respectively. Other books will distinguish between titles, uniform titles, and supplied titles.

The word "title," furthermore, is sometimes used in the special sense of "title proper." The title proper is the first part of a title when a subtitle is present. Thus, if the entire title of a book is *Prison: True Case Histories* the word "Prison" is the title proper.

In the case of a book in the traditional sense, the title is taken from the title page. In other types of publications the title is taken from the equivalent of the title page such as the masthead of a periodical or the printed side of a CD.

It is not always easy to say just which words on a title page comprise the title of the book in hand. A book called *Go in Beauty* has a simple title. There is nothing more to say. But what if the title page reads *Hoyt's Basic Business Methods*? Is "Hoyt's" part of the title? Or is the title "Basic Business Methods"? A simple rule of thumb is to record the fullest form of the title. If it is likely that library users might look under the other part of the title, an added entry can be made. More about title added entries in Chapter 8.

If a publication contains two or three works and has no overall title of its own, the librarian will simply string the titles together:

Going Home ; Man in the Mirror ; Dust and Duty /

The punctuation between titles ("space, semicolon, space," and "space, slash" at the end) is that of the International Standard Bibliographic Description (ISBD), discussed in more detail below.

If the publication contains many works, however, stringing titles together is not practical. Some publishers will pick the title of one of the works and add a descriptive phrase to make a title for the item:

Horseflesh, and other stories

The librarian can adopt the same strategy to make up titles for collections of any kind that have no firm item titles. Here is the title of a compact disc structured that way:

Carnaval, op. 9 [and other music]

The parenthetical statement indicates that other bands on the recording contain different compositions. The brackets (or parentheses, if the typewriter or word processor at hand does not have brackets) indicate that that portion of the title was supplied by the librarian.

Some publications have very long titles. It is sometimes expedient to record a shortened title in such cases, ending with ellipses. Never, however, should one shorten the very beginning of a title. It causes filing and finding problems.

Occasionally a publication contains a work that is known by two titles, such as Beethoven's Sonata in C# minor, op. 27, no. 2, which is also known as Moonlight Sonata. In a scholarly library the official title may be preferred. The bibliographic description then begins with the word "Sonata." The popular title "Moonlight Sonata" can be accessed through a title added entry. In some other type of library it may be better to use the popular title. The word "Moonlight" then leads the bibliographic description, and the official title is relegated to a note.

It is good library practice to record all titles verbatim, word-for-word as shown on the title page. One departure can be recommended: drop the leading article in the nominative case. For speakers of English, where cases have lost their meaning, this is an easy matter: if any English language title begins with the articles a, an, or the, those articles are dropped. If the title of an item is "The Future of Corrections," it becomes "Future of Corrections." Since "The" is not a filing word, dropping it makes finding easier.

Leading articles in other languages are not always so quickly detected. A person who does not know Spanish, for example, will be hard put to distinguish between *Los Burros* (drop "Los," an article in the nominative case) and *Los de Abajo* (do not drop "Los," a pronoun). If, therefore, this rule causes a problem the best policy will be to ignore all English leading articles and to regard all others (and hope that not too many non-English books will find their way into the library).

Some titles of books begin with single letters. Here is a mock title page to illustrate:

B.E.F.
The Whole Story
of the
Bonus Army

Such single letters must be recorded on the card precisely as found on the title page, with periods separating them:

B.E.F.: The whole story of the Bonus Army

This signals to the filer that B, E, and F are separate strings or words, filed as such. Contrast that title with the one that follows:

ABC Algol

Since ABC is written without spaces, or as one string or word, it must be recorded on the card in that way: ABC Algol.

If a title begins with numerals, they must also be recorded on the card in this way. Here is a mock title page:

19
Necromancers
from Now

Here is the corresponding title as recorded on the card: 19 necromancers from now.

If a title begins with a word that is not English but is written in Latin letters it is transcribed as found on the title page, without translation

Dommage, my dear Ernie: a play.

If a non-English title is given in a non-Latin alphabet, however, it must be transliterated into Latin letters before it can be recorded (only transliterated, not translated). Thus, the title shown here 日本現代 … becomes "Nihon gendai. . . ." The cataloger who does not read Japanese must get help, as the author did in this case.

Author Statement

The term "author" includes composers, compilers, editors, translators, and other types of persons and agencies that can be said to be responsible for a publication.

The names of personal authors are given as they appear in the item. Thus, if the title page reads

A
SHORT HISTORY
OF THE
WORLD

H. G. Wells

the author's name in the bibliographic description is given as H. G. Wells. If the author's name is preceded by the word "by" or its equivalent in another language, those words are included in the author statement. Thus, if the title page reads

RED MEN AND WHITE
BY
OWEN WISTER

the author statement following the title in the bibliographic description becomes "by Owen Wister."

Some author situations get very complicated. Consider the following title page:

The Legacy of
GREECE

Essays by Gilbert Murray, W. R. Inge,
J. Burnet, Sir T. L. Heath, D'Arcy W.
Thompson, Charles Singer, R. W.
Livingstone, A. Toynbee, A. E. Zimmern,
Percy Gardner, Sir Reginald Blomfield

Edited by
R. W. Livingstone

The cataloger must first decide where the title ends and where the author statement begins. According to the *Anglo-American Cataloguing Rules*, 2nd ed. (AACR2), the title of this book is *The Legacy of Greece: Essays*. The first part, *The Legacy of Greece*, is called the title proper. The second part, *Essays*, is called "other" title information. This book has two author statements. The first begins with "by Gilbert Murray" and the second is "Edited by R. W. Livingstone." Since the first group of authors consists of more than three names, the author statement in the bibliographic description is shortened to just the first name followed by ellipses and a parenthetic Latin abbreviation indicating that there are others: "by Gilbert Murray. . . [et al.]." Some will prefer to anglicize and make it "by Gilbert Murray [and others]." On the catalog card the two author statements are separated by a semicolon. More on punctuation below. More on the form of authors' names is in Chapter 8.

Names of groups or agencies that are considered to be serving as authors are also given in the bibliographic description as shown on the title page. Thus, if a title page reads

COMPUTERS
by the
Editors of Scientific American

the author statement in the bibliographic description reads "by the editors of Scientific American." If the title page reads

WORKSHOP ON
SOLAR HEATING
Sponsored by
The National Science Foundation

the author statement reads "sponsored by the National Science Foundation." More on corporate authors is in chapter 8.

Whenever the information on the title page is unclear, the cataloger may add necessary words in brackets. If this were the title page,

BEOWULF
Jane Doe

it would be appropriate, since Jane Doe did not write this Anglo-Saxon classic, to give the author statement as "[edited by] Jane Doe."

Edition Statement

This data element is of course needed only for second or subsequent editions of a publication. It is simplest to give the edition in numerical form in a standard format such as "2nd ed.," even if the title page states "Second edition." If the title page states "Revised and greatly enlarged edition," it is sufficient to reduce the edition statement to "rev. ed."

It should be noted that each separately numbered edition of a book is cataloged as a separate item unless the cataloger decides that a so-called open entry record would be more useful. In an open entry no finite date is given, only the date the publication first started, followed by a hyphen, such as "1976-."

Imprint

Typically, this includes place of publication, name of publisher or producer, and date of publication. The imprint information is taken from the title page, front or back, or comparable source of information if the item cataloged is not a book.

The date is usually found on the back of the title page of a book, the verso. Very often more than one date appears. The cataloger should use the latest copyright date. Thus, a book may have been published in 1999, but inspection of the back of the title page reveals that it is the third printing and that the copyright date is 1992. This means that the last time some new information was added to the book was 1992, and it is that date that should be shown in the record.

Some librarians will want to be very technical about this and specify a copyright date by a lowercase "c" prefixed to the date: c1992. Some will even want to give both dates: 1999 (c1992). There is something to be said for simply making it a policy to take the latest copyright date and state it without "c," as in

New York : Appels, 1992.

Occasionally an old book that is in the nature of a classic is reprinted. Frequently such a book carries a new title page that makes it look like a brand new item. The imprint should be based on the new title page, but the fact that it is a reprint of an older edition should be indicated in a note:

(imprint)   New York : Peters, 1982
(note)   Reprint. Originally Boston : Gower, 1881

More about notes can be found below.

In multi-document items the various documents or volumes sometimes have different publication dates. It is best, in such cases, to give the range of dates from the earliest to the latest:

Chicago : Jobes, 1968-1974

Publications that still continue to be published cannot, of course, be given a definite date. Here is the imprint for a typical magazine or periodical, the imprint for an "open entry":

New York: American Heritage Publication Co., 1958-

The hyphen after the year indicates that this is the beginning year of the publication and that it is still being published. Even if the library does not have a complete run going back to the beginning, the imprint date should always be the starting date of the publication. Holdings can be indicated by a note:

Library has 1970-

Some publications are published at irregular intervals. The library may have a policy of acquiring all editions of a certain series as they appear but not wish to make separate catalog entries for each new edition. Open entry is a good stratagem here, too. Instead of cataloging each book separately as "Fodor's Budget Germany 97," "Fodor's Budget Germany 98," "Fodor's Budget Germany 99," and so on, it would be better to create one record for Fodor's Budget Germany . . . (using ellipses instead of the date that appears as part of the title) and indicate the years held by a "Library has" note such as the one that follows:

Library keeps latest edition only

If place of publication and date cannot be determined, as in the case of many nonbook items, the producer's name may be all that can be given in the imprint:

Granada Records.

Such nonbook materials often have unique label numbers that can be used for precise identification. Label numbers can be given in a note. More about that below under "Notes."

THE PHYSICAL DESCRIPTION

The physical description of the item, as opposed to the bibliographic description discussed above, gives the size and dimensions of the item, such as number of pages, number of volumes, length, height, diameter, running time, or other suitable measurement.

In small libraries the physical description, also referred to as the "collation," is often reduced to a minimum. Instead of

xiv, 450 p. :ill., maps ;24cm.

a small library's catalog card may simply say:

450 p.

In other words, only the most essential information is given.
Here is the complete physical description for a three-volume set of books:

3 v. (1633 p.) :ill. ;24cm.

Note that number of volumes and total number of pages are given. A small library may reduce this to

3 v.

For a periodical or other serial the final number of volumes cannot be stated. Here is a way to show that other volumes are to follow:

v. 1-

The beginning volume designation for a periodical is considered in this book to be part of the physical description. Other authorities add this information to the imprint, before the date.

Of course, it is possible to describe a publication without giving any collation. But few libraries practice such austerity because the size of the publication described is often crucial for identification. A reader who remembers that a certain book was very thick will be warned that a similar title given as "58 p." cannot be the desired item.

For some types of publications a medium designation is added to the physical description. If the cataloged item, for example, contains a score or a part, in other words consists primarily of musical symbols, printed on paper, the medium designation "Music" leads the physical description. Materials other than print on paper are also given suitable designations such as "Microform," "Audiocassette," "Compact disc," etc. If an audiovisual item consists of more than one unit this fact can be combined with the medium designation: "2 compact discs." Here is the physical description or collation for a book consisting mostly of printed music:

Music. 110 p.

Here is the physical description for a phonograph record:

1 sound disc :33 1/3 rpm, stereo ;12 in.

This includes medium, playing speed, recording mode, and diameter, in that order. A small library might shorten this, without loss, to

Sound disc, 33 1/3

Since designating the medium of publication is a matter of physical description, this information leads the physical description block. Other writers recommend that the medium information be added to the title in the bibliographic description. By tradition, no medium designation is given for books and periodicals.

NOTES

Any other helpful information not given in the bibliographic or physical description can be added as notes. Here are some examples of notes:

Annals of Mathematics, v.13 (a series note)
Reprint of the 1879 ed.
Liverpool Symphony, George Cox, Conductor (a performer note)
Contents: Beowulf.--Song of Roland.--Kalevala
Library has latest edition only (a holdings note)

In small libraries bibliographic notes are used sparingly because they are not absolutely necessary for the description of an item. But they can be helpful to catalog users.

TRACINGS

This part of the bibliographic record lists all headings or access points other than the title, which leads the bibliographic description. These headings and their tracings will be further discussed under "Added Entries" beginning with Chapter 7.

LOCATION CODE

Chapter 3 deals with this topic, often just referred to as "call number."

PUNCTUATION

The various elements of the bibliographic description—the title, author statement, edition statement, and so forth—can be separated from each other by periods and commas as common sense directs. But the punctuation system of the International Standard Bibliographic Description (ISBD) may be employed to advantage because it standardizes punctuation. The idea is to indicate by punctuation conventions where one element ends and another begins, independent of language. Thus, space-colon-space separates the title proper from other title information, as in:

Dommage, my dear Ernie : a play

Space-slash-space separates the title from the author statement, as in

. . . a play / by Joe Doe

Period-space-double hyphen-space separate the author from the edition statement, as in

by Joe Doe. -- 3rd ed.

and so on. Here is a comprehensive example:

Great victory : the memoirs of a prince / by Fuji Haramake;
transl. by Tom Reid. -- 2nd ed. -- New York : Appels,
1968.

Most sample cards in this book are shown in ISBD form.

Figure 19 is another example of a complete main entry showing all five elements. It is a main entry for a "one-shot" book, an item that is complete in one volume.

Main entry

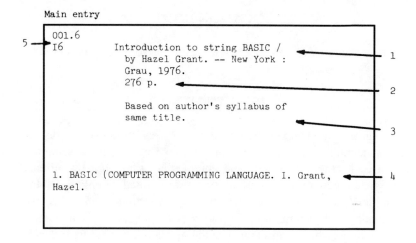

Legend: 1. Bibliographic description (title, author statement, and imprint); 2. Physical description; 3. Note;
4. Tracings; 5. Location code or Call number.

Figure 19. *A title main entry card*

Two other main entries that show all five parts of the description are
pictured in Figures 20 and 21. The first is for a book, an anthology. The
second is for a floppy disk. Notice that the task of cataloging is essentially the same, regardless of the medium of publication.

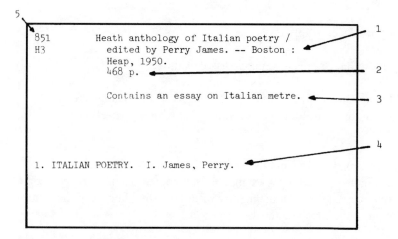

Figure 20. *A title main entry for a book*

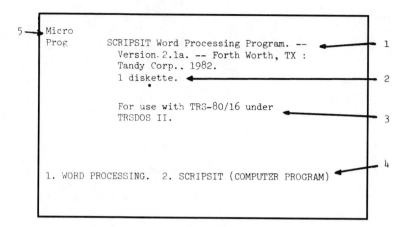

```
5 ─►  Micro
      Prog       SCRIPSIT Word Processing Program. --  ◄───────────  1
                      Version. 2.1a. -- Forth Worth, TX :
                      Tandy Corp.. 1982.
                      1 diskette.  ◄──────────────────────────────  2
                           •

                      For use with TRS-80/16 under
                      TRSDOS II.                      ◄─────────────  3


                                                              ─────  4
      1. WORD PROCESSING.  2. SCRIPSIT (COMPUTER PROGRAM) ◄───
```

Figure 21. *A title main entry for a diskette*

Figure 22 is another main entry, a so-called open entry, made for a set that is not complete but continues to appear periodically. No physical description is given because it varies from issue to issue. The ellipses after the title indicate that there was more information on the title page, in this case "1965/66," "1967/68," and so on. Figure 23 is a main entry without notes.

```
FIN
A6            Almanach of investment information ... --
                  New York : Buspress, 1965-

              Published every other year.
              Numbered on spine: 1-




1. INVESTMENTS.
```

Figure 22. *An open entry*

```
909
L2          Larousse encyclopedia of European history /
            General editor: Joseph Hyslop. -- New
            York : Klamm, 1945.
            508 p.




1. EUROPE--HISTORY.  I. Hyslop, Joseph, ed.
```

Figure 23. *A main entry without notes*

SUMMARY OF STEPS IN MAKING
A MAIN ENTRY RECORD

1. Decide which description principle is appropriate for the item.
2. Devise the location code and type it on the upper left corner of the card or as a note below the physical description.
3. Type bibliographic description, always beginning with the first word of the title that is not an article in the nominative case, in hanging indention format.
4. Directly below, or leaving a line free if space permits, type the physical description in a paragraph or block that is not indented. This block is sometimes referred to as the collation.
5. Below the physical description, type any necessary notes in paragraphs that are not indented.
6. After deciding what added entries are needed (see Chapter 7 and further), type appropriate tracings across the bottom of the card. The result is a complete title main entry.

USING CIP TO CREATE A MAIN ENTRY

Many new books today carry what is known as "Cataloging-in-publication," or CIP. This is catalog card information printed on the back, or verso, of the title page. The Library of Congress generates this information on the basis of galley proofs submitted by publishers. CIP data can greatly simplify the small library cataloger's life. Here is an example:

Beakley, George C.
Design: serving the needs of man.
Based on the author's Introduction to engineering design and graphics.
1. Engineering design. I. Chilton, Ernest G., joint author. II. Title.
TA174.B39   620.0042   73-2762
ISBN 0-02-307240-7

When the library buys a book like this, the CIP information can be used to generate a deck of cards. Imprint and physical description, of course, have to be taken from the book itself. The numbers below the tracings, incidentally, are the Library of Congress call number (TA174.B39), the Dewey decimal classification number (620.0042), the Library of Congress control number (73-2762), and the International standard book number or ISBN (0-02-307240-7).

CATALOG INFORMATION FROM THE INTERNET

The Internet, too, can be of help to the cataloger. World Wide Web and Telnet connections to hundreds of library catalogs are now available to anyone with a 486+ PC, a modem, a browser, and an access provider like Earthlink, AOL, or such. Most catalog information captured in this way will be in the form of a MARC record, described in some detail in Chapter 16.

Chapter Seven

Preparing Catalog Cards: Added Entries

The title main entry record is filed, of course, under the first word of the title as typed in the bibliographic description. This is a satisfactory access point for the library user who is looking for the publication in the catalog under that first word of the title. The reader looking for Grant's book *Introduction to String BASIC* will find it by looking under the word "introduction." But how about the reader who is looking for the book on BASIC by Grant, or the library patron who just needs information on BASIC?

The answer is quite simple. The cataloger makes additional records, called added entries, that are filed under different access points. To provide access by author or by an alternate form of the title, author added entries and title added entries are made. These are discussed in detail in Chapter 8. To provide access by subject or other categories, subject added entries are made, discussed in Chapter 9.

The reader should notice that on added entries, as on the main entry, only the bibliographic description paragraph is indented. All other paragraphs are typed straight, without indentions. The tracings are usually omitted on added entries when the cards are individually typed. Figure 24 is a schematic of the format.

Added entry records are essentially copies of the main entry record with different headings typed across the top. This practice is sometimes referred to as the unit card system of cataloging. The advantage for users is that they find complete information about the item no matter under what heading they may have found it. Figure 25 is an example of a subject added entry based on a unit card. The tracings and notes are omitted.

Added entry

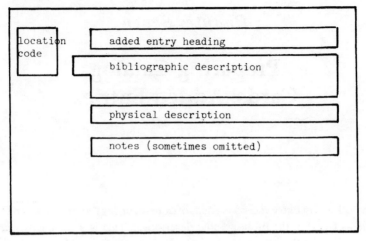

Figure 24. *Schematic of an added entry card*

Added entry

```
001.6         BASIC (COMPUTER PROGRAMMING LANGUAGE)
I6
              Introduction to string BASIC / by
              Hazel Grant. -- New York : Grau,
              1976.
              276 p.
```

Added
entry
heading

Figure 25. *A subject added entry card*

In libraries where cards are typed individually (rather than run off automatically from data stored in a PC, for example) the staff often skimps on the typing and does not repeat the complete unit card record on each added entry. To a point, such economy is reasonable. But it should stop at the bibliographic description. Even a shortened added entry should always repeat at least the bibliographic description exactly as given on the main entry. This preserves the unit card principle, essentially, which is a great help when it comes to catalog maintenance and library housekeeping. Compare the added entry shown in Figure 25 with the shortened version found in Figure 26. On such an abbreviated card the user is given no clue as to who wrote it, what edition, how old, how big, etc. A frustrating sort of catalog.

A note concerning terminology: The term "added entry," according to the *ALA Glossary*, definition 2, designates any bibliographic record additional to the main entry record. This is the meaning of added entry throughout this book. Many librarians, however, distinguish between added entries and subject entries. If that narrower definition is accepted, the term added entry comprises only author and title added entries.

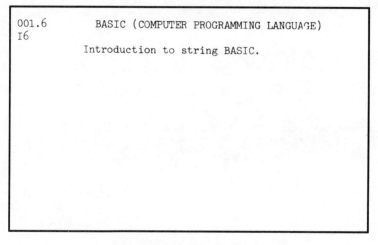

```
001.6        BASIC (COMPUTER PROGRAMMING LANGUAGE)
I6
             Introduction to string BASIC.
```

Figure 26. *A short added entry*

Chapter Eight

Author and Title Added Entries

PERSONAL AUTHOR ENTRIES

Suppose a publication is to be cataloged following the "title main entry" system advocated here, and this publication contains only one work
and has one person named as author. For this publication an author
added entry must be made. Figure 27 is an example. This author added
entry is filed in the catalog under "Lew." If a publication contains many
works by one author it also requires an author added entry. The card in
Figure 28 is an example.

Added entry

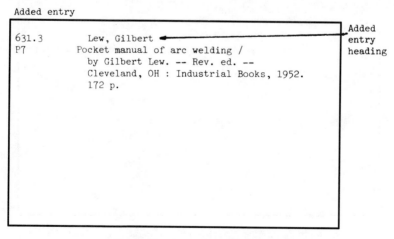

```
631.3        Lew, Gilbert  ◄───────────        Added
P7           Pocket manual of arc welding /                 entry
             by Gilbert Lew. -- Rev. ed. --                 heading
             Cleveland, OH : Industrial Books, 1952.
             172 p.
```

Figure 27. *An author added entry*

```
LIT          Doe, Joe
D7
             Six contemporary plays / by Joe
             Doe. -- New York : Holst, 1990.
```

Figure 28. *An author added entry for many works by the same author*

If a publication contains many works by different authors, those authors are not usually singled out by added entries. Instead, an added entry may be made for the editor or compiler. If an added entry is made for an editor, compiler, or translator, the resulting entry is still called an "author" entry, as shown in Figure 29.

```
520.1        Gluck, Hanna
P7
             Progress in astronomy / edited by
             Hanna Gluck. -- London : Astronomical
             Society, 1988.
```

Figure 29. *An author added entry for editor, compiler, or translator of many works by different authors*

If a publication contains one work written in cooperation by several persons, separate added entry records should be prepared for all authors. But if the list of cooperating authors or editors gets too long (more than three, perhaps) most libraries refrain from making added entries for any but the first named. From a point of logic this makes no sense, but it is defensible on practical, economic grounds.

Nonbooks

It is possible, even likely, that some of the publications cataloged in a small library are not books. They may be periodicals, pamphlets, or cassettes. For the cataloger, the distinction between books and nonbooks is of no consequence. A publication, any type of publication, is represented in the catalog by a title main entry. If the publication has a personal author in the extended bibliographic sense, including an editor, translator, performer or such, a personal author added entry is made for that publication. The example shown in Figure 30 is the author added entry for the composer of the music recorded on a CD. The composer's full name makes up the author added entry heading.

While the label on the record gives the composer's name simply as "Grieg," the cataloger must supply the full name in the catalog heading to prevent confusion with authors that have identical surnames. Once

```
PHONO       Grieg, Edvard Hagerup
242         Norwegian dances, op. 35 : [and other
            music] / [by] Grieg. -- Vixen.

            Sound disc : digital ; 4 3/4 in.

            Vixen CD 23435-2
```

Figure 30. *An author added entry for a composer of the music recorded on a CD*

the form of a name has been established, it should always be used in the same form throughout the catalog.

Which Name?

Occasionally an author is known by more than one name. Standard practice in libraries today is to put into the author heading that name by which the person is commonly known. Thus it should not be Carter, James Earl; Thibault, Jacques-Anatole; or Clemens, Samuel Langhorne. Instead we use Carter, Jimmy; France, Anatole; and Twain, Mark. The catalog will be easiest to use if all the works of an author are listed under the same name. To maintain consistency a separate authority file may be kept, where each name that occurs in the catalog is recorded on a card. Cross references to this "official" or "authorized" name can be made from the author's other name or names as needed (cross references are explained in Chapter 12).

Distinguishing between Identical Names

As catalogs grow larger it happens that different authors are encountered who have identical names. It is then necessary to add dates to names for precise identification:

Smith, Jim, 1926-
Smith, Jim, 1949-

Such additional information should be recorded in the catalog as well as in the authority file.

Name Changes

From time to time one finds an author who has changed his or her name. There is no fixed standard procedure for handling such situations, but a good basic rule is to use the new name throughout, changing all old name headings that may be already in the catalog. If changing cards is for some really compelling reason not possible an alternative method would be to insert into the catalog a so-called "see also" cross reference from the old name to the current name so that readers don't miss out when looking for a given author's works. But the result will be a confusing catalog. Any name changes should, of course, also be reflected in the authority file.

Form of Personal Author Heading

If an author's name consists of more than one part, such as a given name and a surname, that part of the name is typed first by which the added entry is to be filed. This is known as a question of "form of heading." Notice that in the first example in this chapter Gilbert Lew's name was inverted for the heading and typed as "Lew, Gilbert." Inversion of the name has the effect of arranging all such entries under the surnames.

Names with separately written prefixes can pose problems for the cataloger. A good basic rule is to treat all prefixes as part of the name. Thus the author heading for John van der Mitten appears as Van der Mitten, John. The heading for Beulah de Los Grandes is De Los Grandes, Beulah. The heading for the corporate author Los Altos City Museum is just that, Los Altos City Museum. Unfortunately, customs vary from country to country and it is not always easy to know if the prefix should be part of the name or not; should it be Bodlien, Gertrud von, for example, or Von Bodlien, Gertrud? The cataloger may have to consult reference sources and possibly make cross references from the form of the name not used.

Care must also be taken with double names. The American writer John Rowe Ransom is entered as "Ransom, John Rowe." But the British statesman David Lloyd George becomes "Lloyd George, David." Spanish names often present similar difficulties. The poet Federico Garcia Lorca, very often just referred to as "Lorca," is actually "Garcia Lorca, Federico." But Juan Nicasio Gallego is "Gallego, Juan Nicasio." In case of doubt, biographical reference sources must be consulted to establish the correct form of a name.

CORPORATE AUTHOR ENTRIES

Some publications are issued by corporate agencies rather than by individually named people. The example in Figure 31 is a so-called corporate author added entry. It is made for the benefit of library users who

Added entry (corporate author)

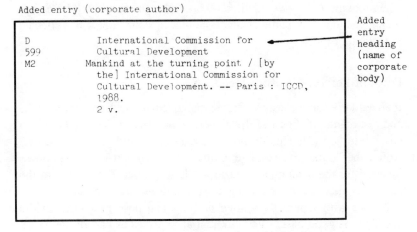

```
D              International Commission for  ◄─────        Added
599            Cultural Development                         entry
M2             Mankind at the turning point / [by          heading
               the] International Commission for           (name of
               Cultural Development. -- Paris : ICCD,       corporate
               1988.                                        body)
               2 v.
```

Figure 31. *A corporate author added entry*

might know only the name of the issuing agency or who want to know which publications of this organization are owned by the library.

Form of Corporate Author Headings

On the question of form in corporate author headings whole chapters could be written. Suffice it to say that there are two ways to construct a corporate name heading. One can take the name as it is presented in the publication itself on the title page and show it in that form in the added entry heading. This may lead to inconsistent entries in the catalog, however, because different publications by the same agency may not show the agency's name in the same form every time.

A second method is to show the name of the agency in a standardized form, regardless of how it is presented in the publication. Such standardized corporate names often are laid out in a hierarchical pattern. A government agency's name, for example, usually begins with the name of the jurisdiction, followed by the names of lesser units:

New York (City). Police Department.

or

United States. Congress. Senate. Committee on the Judiciary. Subcommittee on Federal Charters, Holidays, and Celebrations.

The entire two lines in the last example are one agency's name. A helpful book for determining the hierarchical relationships among various agencies of the United States government is the annual *United States Government Manual* published by the Office of the Federal Register and sold by the Government Printing Office, Washington, DC 20402.

Sometimes the full name of a corporate agency is divided into so many sub-agencies that one may want to eliminate the middle portion of the name, giving only the largest unit followed by the smallest subdivision that can stand alone without being confused with another agency. Thus, instead of writing "North Carolina. Department of Transportation. Division of Highways" one may use the simpler heading "North Carolina. Division of Highways," there being only one Division of Highways in the state of North Carolina. The most important principle in establishing corporate author headings is consistency. If a name is once established as, say, "New York (City). Police Department," then all publications emanating from that department should be kept together under the same heading. If the principle of consistency is disregarded in the catalog and in the authority file, police department documents will soon become widely dispersed under such headings as "City of New York. Police Department," "Police Department of the City of New York," "New York Police," and other possible variants of the name.

Entry of publications under jurisdictions, such as North Carolina. Division of Highways, is going out of fashion. Whenever a name can stand alone it should be used without the name of the superior agency. Thus it is "Library of Congress," not "United States. Library of Congress."

Often the official name of an organization is not widely known. An example is the Teamsters' Union. The full name of that body is "International Brotherhood of Teamsters, Chauffeurs, Warehousemen and Helpers of America." Such a name deserves a cross reference like the one shown as Figure 32. More on cross-references in Chapter 12.

Figure 32. *A cross-reference card*

Corporate Author Plus Uniform Title

In some fields, such as law and political science, it often happens that publications of a certain type must be assembled in the catalog under the name of a jurisdiction and further arranged by type of publication, as for example "laws" in a legal library or a corporate library. The type of law, in such a library, becomes a uniform title which is added to the heading as a second added entry paragraph under the name of the jurisdiction as corporate author, in brackets. Inclusion of uniform titles in this fashion insures that all editions of the California agricultural code, for example, stand together in the catalog, no matter what the actual titles of the editions may be.

Figure 33 shows other examples of corporate author plus uniform title added entries and how they keep certain types of works together in the catalog. Suppose there were three books in the library containing the constitution of the United States, entitled, respectively, *Our Constitution*, *America's Basic Law*, and *Understanding the Constitution*. Figure 34 shows the added entries, all three together. If it makes for simpler typing, the author/title heading can of course also be placed on one line:

United States [Constitution]

This would not affect the filing and finding.

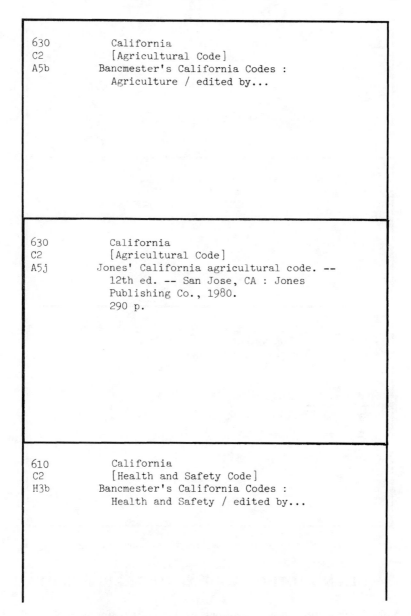

```
630          California
C2           [Agricultural Code]
A5b          Bancmester's California Codes :
             Agriculture / edited by...
```

```
630          California
C2           [Agricultural Code]
A5j          Jones' California agricultural code. --
             12th ed. -- San Jose, CA : Jones
             Publishing Co., 1980.
             290 p.
```

```
610          California
C2           [Health and Safety Code]
H3b          Bancmester's California Codes :
             Health and Safety / edited by...
```

Figure 33. *Examples showing use of uniform titles*

```
KF              United States
4525            [Constitution]
G6              America's basic law / [ed. by]
                Joe Doe. -- New York : Glaubers,
                1970.
```

```
KF              United States
4527            [Constitution]
L2              Our constitution / by Jane Allin. --
                Boston : Lance Publications, 1975.
```

```
KF              United States
2528            [Constitution]
B8              Understanding the constitution /
                [by] Enid Brock. -- Chicago :
                Folley, 1967.
```

Figure 34. *More examples showing use of uniform titles*

WHEN NO AUTHOR ADDED ENTRIES ARE NEEDED

Not all publications need author entries. Periodicals, for example, such as *Time* or the *New Yorker*, cannot be said to have personal authors and no author added entries are made, regardless of how well known the editor may be.

TITLE ADDED ENTRIES

Uniform Title Entries

Occasionally the title given on the title page of a publication, and therefore leading the bibliographic description, the "natural" title, is not what library users are likely to look for. Whenever different editions of a work bear different titles, it may be necessary to collect them together in the catalog by a uniform title.

The Bible is a type of book that requires a uniform title added entry so that all versions may be kept together. Consider the example shown in Figure 35. Few people would look for it in the catalog under H for Holy; instead, they will look for the uniform title "Bible." With the uniform title the cataloger brings together all the versions of the Bible that the library may own, regardless of whether the books are entitled *Holy Bible, New English Bible, Modern Bible,* or whatever.

Literary works often need uniform titles. Take the case of *The Tragedy of Hamlet Prince of Denmark* by William Shakespeare. Not many library patrons will look for this book under T for Tragedy. Instead they will look for the shortened popular or "uniform" title, "Hamlet." That is why an added entry for that uniform title is made, in the same format used for author added entries, as shown in Figures 36 and 37. By this stratagem all editions of the play are listed together in the catalog, as shown in Figure 38. The uniform title also keeps together the English and the original French editions of the play shown in the Figure 39.

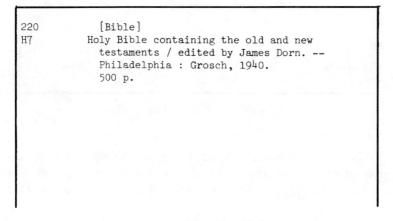

```
220         [Bible]
H7          Holy Bible containing the old and new
            testaments / edited by James Dorn. --
            Philadelphia : Grosch, 1940.
            500 p.
```

Figure 35. *A uniform title added entry*

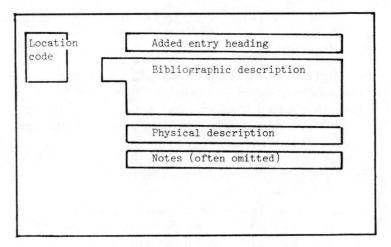

Figure 36. *Schematic for a title added entry*

```
822.33      [Hamlet]
H2          Tragedy of Hamlet, Prince of Denmark /
D7            by William Shakespeare ; ed. by Joe
            Doe. -- Chicago : Willaman, 1920.
            200 p.
```

Figure 37. *A uniform title added entry*

When it comes to literary classics library patrons often expect all versions of a title to be collocated under the author's name as well. For Shakespeare's plays, to elaborate on the earlier example, it may be a

```
PR
2807       Hamlet and Julius Caesar : two
X7            Shakespearean tragedies for the
              modern reader... 1980.


PR         [Hamlet]
2807       Tragedy of Hamlet, Prince of Denmark /
Y6            by William Shakespeare ; ed. by...
              1970.


PR
2807       Hamlet / William Shakespeare. --
Z5            London : Agee, 1958.
```

Figure 38. *An interfiled uniform title card*

good idea to make author/uniform title added entry cards with headings like these:

Shakespeare, William, [Hamlet]
Shakespeare, William, [Richard III]

and so on. This stratagem will ensure that readers looking for Shakespeare's "Hamlet" or his "Richard the Third," "King Richard III," "Tragedy of Richard the Third," "First quarto of King Richard the Third," or however the play may have been entitled in the various books the library owns, will find them neatly collocated or grouped together in the card tray.

```
842              [Huis clos]
S2               No exit / Jean-paul Sartre ; tr. by
H7e              Joe Doe. -- New York : Crofts, 1980.

842
S2               Huis clos / Jean-Paul Sartre. --
H7               Paris : Proche, 1970.
```

Figure 39. *A natural and a uniform title, filed adjacently*

Uniform titles are not phenomena that occur in the real world of books. Uniform titles are not found on the title pages of books. They are made up by librarians on the basis of presumed reader needs and certain conventions. There are few generally binding principles. Catalogers make these decisions from case to case, supported by precedent as found in previous cataloging, reference books, bibliographies, rule books, and other libraries' catalogs. As in all other phases of cataloging, consistency is of the essence in the establishment of uniform titles. The cataloger who decides to enter one of Shakespeare's plays under the uniform title should be consistent and do it for all of Shakespeare's plays whose natural titles begin with non-significant words. If "Tragedy of Hamlet" becomes [Hamlet], then "First Part of King Henry the Fourth" might become [Henry IV, Part 1] and "Comedy of Much Ado about Nothing" could turn into [Much Ado about Nothing], and so on. Notice, though, that an edition of Hamlet that has the natural title "Hamlet" does not also need the uniform title [Hamlet].

By convention uniform titles are enclosed in brackets to indicate that the information was supplied by the cataloger. It should also be mentioned that a uniform title supplements the natural title. It does not take its place, no matter how unlikely it may be that readers will look for the natural title.

Keyword Title Entries

Some natural titles begin with nondistinctive words, such as "Introduction to . . ." or "Dictionary of . . .," that are often not exactly remembered by library users. Keywords that appear further inside the title, however, are more easily remembered. This is why it is sometimes a good idea to make added entries for keyword titles. Figure 40 is an example.

TRACINGS

All added entries must be traced on the main entry. Author tracings are by convention numbered in Roman numerals. Thus, the tracing for the added entry shown as Figure 28, above, might read:

I. Lew, Gilbert.

```
001.6        String BASIC
I6           Introduction to string BASIC / by
             Hazel Grant. -- New York : Grau,
             1976.
```

Figure 40. *A title added entry card*

The tracing for the corporate author added entry shown as Figure 32, above, might read:

I. International Commission for Cultural Development.

Here is the tracing for the topmost heading shown in Figure 34:

I. California [Agricultural Code]

The reason for tracings is this: once an added entry is made and filed away, it passes out of the cataloger's consciousness unless a careful record is maintained. And since it is highly undesirable to have unknown and uncontrolled entries in the catalog, a complete record of all added entries is kept on each main entry. By means of this record the cataloger can trace all added entries, whence the name "tracings" for this bit of housekeeping information kept on the main entry. If the last copy of a book is removed from the library by loss or weeding, the main entry must be removed from the catalog, of course. The tracings at the foot of the main entry remind the cataloger to pull all added entries out of the catalog as well, or to "pull the tracings," as the jargon goes. If this step is forgotten, blind references remain in the catalog, cards for which there are no books. Each tracing, by the way, repeats verbatim the information that has been given in the added entry heading.

Complete and reliable records must be kept for title added entries, too. For each title added entry that is made a suitable tracing is added at the foot of the main entry. Title tracings follow author tracings. They are numbered in Roman numerals with the word "Title:" added. Figure 41 shows two main entries complete with tracings.

```
220
H7        Holy Bible containing the old and new
             testaments / edited by James Dorn. --
             Philadelphia : Grosch, 1940.
          500 p.




I. Dorn, James, ed.  II. Title: [Bible]
```

```
001.6
I6          Introduction to string BASIC / by
               Hazel Grant. -- New York : Grau,
            1976.




1. BASIC (COMPUTER PROGRAM LANGUAGE)  I. Grant,
Hazel.  II. Title: String BASIC.
```

Figure 41. *Tracings*

Chapter Nine

Categorical Added Entries: Subject and Form Headings

Author and title added entries serve those library users who are looking for a publication of which they know the author or the title. Many library users, however, take a different approach. They will be looking for any suitable publication on a certain subject or of a certain kind. They do not know the names of authors or the titles of any particular publications. They look for publications that fall into certain categories. A different kind of added entry is provided for such readers. We call it here a categorical added entry. There are three kinds of categorical added entries: subject added entries (what a work is about, such as a book about raising orchids), genre added entries (the form of a work, such as a play or a novel), and format added entries (the kind of thing a book is, such as an atlas or a dictionary). All three kinds of categorical added entries are often referred to as "subject headings," a traditional, if inexact term.

SUBJECT ADDED ENTRIES

Most categorical entries are made for the subject of books. All books (and of course also all other media) that have to do with, say, organic chemistry can be described by an added entry that carries a suitable subject term, such as

CHEMISTRY, ORGANIC

in the added entry heading, as in the example shown in Figure 42. By convention, subject headings are typed in all uppercase letters.

Added entry (subject)

```
                                                        Added
                                                        entry
615.3        CHEMISTRY, ORGANIC  ◄──────────────        heading
C7           Chemistry of organic medical products /    (subject
             by Glenn L. Jenkins [and] Walter           heading)
             Herting. -- 3rd ed. -- New York :
             Culver, 1975.
             499 p.
```

Figure 42. *A subject added entry card*

Another example would be the book entitled *Barrow, Pyramid, and Tomb*, by Leslie V. Grinsell. It deals with tombs. A subject added entry might be made under the heading TOMBS. For readers who are looking for a slightly different aspect of the subject, another added entry can be made for the same book under the subject heading FUNERAL RITES AND CEREMONIES.

However, subject terminology used in headings must be controlled to remain useful. It will not do to simply invent subject headings on the spot. There are too many words in the English language to guarantee any semblance of consistency and uniformity in an uncontrolled subject heading vocabulary. The same cataloger working on the book by Grinsell, for example, could on another day have assigned the heading GRAVES. To a similar book the heading CRYPTS might be given. A prospective reader interested in burial practices would never find all the relevant books unless he or she could think of all similar headings. To prevent scattering of related materials under different terms many libraries control their subject heading vocabulary by using a published general schedule such as the *Sears List of Subject Headings* or the *Library of Congress Subject Headings*. Many specialized lists are available also, such as *Medical Subject Headings*, published by the National Library of Medicine, the *Thesaurus of Engineering and Scientific Terms*, published by the Engineers Joint Council, the *INSPEC The-*

saurus, published by the British Institution of Electrical Engineers, and many others. Here is a sample entry copied from the *Sears List of Subject Headings*:

Tombs 726
    See also Brasses; Catacombs; Cemeteries; Epitaphs; Mounds and Mound builders
    x Burial; Graves; Mausoleums; Rock tombs; Sepulchers; Vaults (Sepulchral)
    xx Archeology; Architecture; Cemeteries; Monuments; Shrines

This entry tells the cataloger that Tombs is an approved subject heading. The number 726 is the suggested Dewey Decimal Classification section for tombs. The *see also* paragraph suggests to the cataloger that the five headings listed, Brasses, Catacombs, Cemeteries, Epitaphs, and Mounds and Mound builders, might be considered instead of Tombs, for the book in hand.

The *see also*, x, and xx paragraphs in the *Sears List* example have to do with cross-references, references from certain headings to other headings in the catalog. Cross-references will be discussed in Chapter 12.

Occasionally, printed subject heading lists contain scope notes to help the cataloger choose the proper heading. Here is an example, also from the *Sears List*:

Maps 912
Use for general materials about maps and their history.

Materials on the methods of map making and the mapping of areas are entered under Map drawing. Collections of maps of several countries are entered under Atlases. Here is an entry copied from the *INSPEC Thesaurus*:

Internal combustion engines
NT   two cycle engines
BT   engines
RT   ignition
        starting

The abbreviations stand for narrower term (NT), broader term (BT), and related term (RT). The idea is to help the cataloger select the best fitting subject heading for the book in hand. Thesauri also sometimes add scope notes. This example is from *INSPEC Thesaurus*:

mechanical variables control
this heading is restricted to those variables which are not covered by other specific headings. See also, for example, force control; thickness control; velocity control; vibration control.

The *Sears List* heading "Maps" shown above is a single-word heading. But because of the fine nuances of meaning in the English language, many subjects must be expressed in several words. Here are some examples: GLASS FIBERS, FORCE AND ENERGY, FORGERY OF WORKS OF ART, GRANTS-IN-AID, BLACKS IN LITERATURE AND ART. Single-word and multi-word headings can be in the singular (FOOTBALL, GLASS FIBER) or, often with different meaning, in the plural (TOMBS, GLASS FIBERS).

By convention, some multi-word headings are given in direct order (MUNICIPAL FINANCE, AMERICAN LITERATURE), others are inverted (FINANCE, PERSONAL, OR ART, AMERICAN). Some multi-word headings are given as phrases (ART INDUSTRIES AND TRADE), others consist of a heading with a subdivision (ART—GALLERIES AND MUSEUMS). Such inconsistencies occur in many lists of subject headings. They must be dealt with as they occur. They cannot be "learned" since there is no logic behind them.

When using lists of subject descriptors such as the *Thesaurus of Engineering and Scientific Terms* already mentioned above, the cataloger finds that many terms in such lists are single concept terms. Consider a book that explains how to fly a helicopter. In the *Sears List of Subject Headings* a conveniently precoordinated heading will be found that expresses the subject of the book in one term: HELICOPTERS—PILOTING. In the *Thesaurus of Engineering and Scientific Terms*, however, there is no such heading. The cataloger will probably do best by assigning two separate terms, HELICOPTERS and PILOT TRAINING. One card, then, will be filed under H, the other under P. The person looking for material on flying helicopters can look under HELICOPTERS and scan all the titles listed there for books that deal with piloting, or else look under PILOT TRAINING and see if any books

```
629          HELICOPTERS
F5           Flying the HFG-200 helicopter :
             a manual for student pilots /
             by George Doe. -- New York :
             Grey, 1988.
             399 p.



1. HELICOPTERS.  2. PILOT TRAINING.  I. Doe,
George.
```

Figure 43. *A subject added entry card*

specifically devoted to helicopters are listed. If tracings are maintained on all entries, the catalog user can simplify the search by scanning all tracings for the companion term. Figure 43 shows the picture of a card that would lead to a relevant book in this fictitious search.

Even with the help of published lists, however, the assignment of subject headings to publications is very difficult work. In one large American library the fifth edition of a book entitled *Abnormal Psychology and Modern Life*, for example, was given the subject heading PSYCHIATRY. But the sixth edition of the same book cannot be found under that heading. It was entered under PSYCHOLOGY, PATHOLOGICAL. This shows how difficult it is to be consistent, even for highly skilled and experienced librarians.

Not all publications have a subject. Beethoven's Pastoral Symphony recorded in a publication called RCA Victor LM 2114, for example, is neither about pastors nor about symphonies. It is not about music, either. It is not about anything; it simply *is* music. Such a publication needs no subject heading.

Also, not all subjects are topics. A book about the painter Henri Matisse, for example, is not about something but about someone. It needs a subject heading like this:

MATISSE, HENRI

Since it is hard to predict about whom books will be written, there is, of course, no published master list of name subject headings. The cataloger makes them up on the spot, taking care to be consistent in form and spelling. Thus, if a book about Igor Chernov gets the subject heading CHERNOV, IGOR, then a second book about the same person should have the same heading, not some variant such as TCHERNOV or CHERNOW.

Some books are about other books. Typically, the subject heading for such an item consists of the name of the author plus the title of the book that is the subject. A book discussing Darwin's *Origin of Species* gets this subject heading:

DARWIN, CHARLES ROBERT, 1809-1882. ON THE ORIGIN OF SPECIES BY MEANS OF NATURAL SELECTION.

Such author/title subject headings, too, will not be found in any list. They must be made up as needed and this should be done in a consistent fashion. The same goes for uniform title subject headings. A book about the Bible, for example, gets the subject heading BIBLE. But it should be noted that a book entitled *The New American Bible*, containing the text of the Bible, gets a title added entry under the heading "Bible." It does not get a subject added entry under BIBLE because it is not *about* the Bible: it *is* the Bible.

Like classification, subject heading work requires a thorough understanding of the field of knowledge represented by the library's collection. There is no shortcut possible because the task requires two fundamental steps that cannot be simplified: first, an examination of the publication in hand to determine what it is about (which takes knowledge and experience), and second, the selection of suitable terms to express the subject content in such a way that all publications dealing in a similar way with the same topics will always carry the same subject headings and that the headings chosen are the best ones for the library's clientele (which takes more knowledge, experience, and a thorough familiarity with the schedule of headings used, with the library's holdings, and with the needs of the library's users).

If the cataloger lacks the subject knowledge or necessary experience and cannot enlist the help of an expert, it is far better to defer the making of subject added entries, or even to abandon the project altogether, than to waste time and energy on the childish exercise of listing, in a medical library, a book entitled *Introduction to the Medical Profession* under the subject heading MEDICINE, or in a church library, a book on St. Paul under RELIGION. Far better not to have a subject catalog than a poorly done subject catalog that lists books under topics and aspects of topics that they don't really deal with, or fails to list important publications under the key subjects that they do deal with.

However, the person appointed to operate a small library often has no power in such decisions. Administrators, having little expertise as far as library work is concerned, cannot be relied upon to appreciate the complexities of subject cataloging. To them it seems a simple task that has to be done. A compromise solution must therefore be found. Here are a few pointers, then, on how to go about assigning subject headings to books and other publications.

First, adopt a published master list of subject headings. Get help and advice from the American Library Association, the Special Libraries Association, the Medical Library Association, or any other suitable professional organization in the field. The *Bowker Annual* mentioned in Chapter 2 can be helpful here.

Second, take the publication to be cataloged and study the table of contents (if it is a book), the label (if it is a compact disc, phonograph record, cassette, or similar medium), the preface, introduction, blurb, or whatever summary information about the publication is available. Determine if the publication can be said to be "about" anything.

Third, if a publication can be said to have a subject, determine if the whole publication is about one well-defined subject, or about several separate subjects, or about several sub-topics of one general subject. If the publication contains several distinct works, determine if they all deal with the same subject or with several separate subjects.

Fourth, if the publication deals with one subject assign to it from the master list the narrowest term that characterizes the subject. Thus, a book devoted entirely to the behavior of sheep is given the narrow subject heading

SHEEP--BEHAVIOR

not the broad heading SHEEP. The cataloger must avoid assigning general subject headings in addition to specific ones. A book dealing with the history of twentieth-century sculpture carries one specific heading

SCULPTURE--HISTORY--20TH CENTURY

It should not also be listed under SCULPTURE--HISTORY and under SCULPTURE. The entries would file close to each other, leading to unnecessary redundancy.

Fifth, if the publication or the works contained in it deal with a small number of separate subjects for which no comprehensive term exists, assign the narrowest possible term for each of the components of the topic. Thus for a book about sheep and swine assign two headings, SHEEP and SWINE, since there is no collective name for these two kinds of animals.

Sixth, a book dealing with many sub-topics of a general topic poses a problem. Consider a book dealing with bricks, cement, concrete, stone, structural steel, wallboard, and wood, in so many chapters. A subject entry could be made under the heading BRICKS. But this would be misleading since the book does not deal with one sole subject, bricks. Only one chapter is about bricks. A better, more logical strategy is to enter this book under a summary term that comprises bricks, cement, concrete, etc. One term that covers all these materials would be

BUILDING MATERIALS

Of course, this broad summary heading does not help the person with a special interest in bricks. For that reader a so-called subject analytic added entry would be fine, under the heading

BRICKS, chapter 1 of

The analytic tells the reader exactly what to expect: only one chapter in the book is on bricks. Needless to say, such analytics are costly in time taken for design, production, and filing. They are therefore seldom made. But more on analytics in Chapter 10.

Often so much material accumulates under a heading that it must be subdivided to provide a finer breakdown of the topic. Subject headings are often subdivided by other subjects (PHILOSOPHY--HISTORY).

They can also be subdivided by region (ART--ITALY), by genre (ITALY--FICTION), or by format (LINGUISTICS--ATLASES). History headings are often more complex. History books are first divided into countries or regions, subdivided by the word "History":

EUROPE--HISTORY
UNITED STATES--HISTORY

For finer distinctions, history is then divided into time periods by means of so-called chronological subdivisions. Chronological subdivisions, published as all other subdivisions in the *Sears List* and in similar aids, are tailored to the country under discussion. The years 1492 and 1648, for example, are important landmarks in the history of Europe. Books dealing with historical aspects of the Renaissance and the Reformation, therefore, may be assigned a three-part subject heading, like:

EUROPE--HISTORY--1492-1648

That same time period is not meaningful in the context of the history of the United States. Here, books might deal with the Revolution:

UNITED STATES--HISTORY--REVOLUTION, 1775-1783

Revolutions, of course, have happened elsewhere, but at different times. Thus the catalog may have other headings that follow the same pattern:

FRANCE--HISTORY--REVOLUTION, 1791-1797
ITALY--HISTORY--REVOLUTION OF 1848

Occasionally, still further refinements are needed, such as:

ITALY--HISTORY--REVOLUTION OF 1848--FICTION

But small libraries ought to keep headings as simple as possible. Often the only reason for subdivisions is to divide large blocks of like headings into meaningful groups. If the library has only a few things on a topic, two- and three-part headings are a nuisance to the catalog user, not a help.

To sum up: a subject heading answers the question, Is this a publication or work about something or someone?

GENRE ADDED ENTRIES

Some books are looked for because they contain literature of a certain genre. Figure 44 shows a genre added entry for a collection of stories. Since the heading here designates the genre of literature contained in the book cataloged, not the subject of the book, this type of heading cannot rightly be called a subject heading. It would best be called a genre heading.

Genre added entries are easier to make than subject added entries because the available choice of terms is much smaller. There is only a very limited number of genres to be considered. But genre headings, too, must be controlled to prevent inconsistency. Published lists of subject headings can be used for guidance. They usually contain many genre headings. This fact is not well advertised, although the distinction between subject and genre is often made. The 12th edition of the *Sears List of Subject Headings*, for example, has this entry under SHORT STORY:

SHORT STORY 808.3
    Use for materials on the technique of short story
    writing. Collections of short stories are entered
    under SHORT STORIES

```
808.83        SHORT STORIES
W7            World treasury of short fiction /
                ed. by Joe Doe. -- Boston :
                Gremlin, 1921.
                480 p.
```

Figure 44. *A genre added entry card*

Clearly, this note implies a difference between subject and genre heading, even if the nature of the difference is not spelled out. Unfortunately, the distinction is not carried through consistently. Thus there are no term pairs like poetry/poems or drama/plays in the *Sears List*. For uniformity and clarity it is recommended that, in literature, plain headings be interpreted as genre headings. Let SHORT STORIES be assigned to a publication that contains short stories. Let AMERICAN POETRY be assigned to an anthology of American poetry. Let DRAMA be assigned to a book that contains plays.

Should a book, however, contain essays about the drama or about individual plays, use the heading with a suitable subdivision:

DRAMA--HISTORY AND CRITICISM

Likewise, the heading GERMAN POETRY stands for a book that contains poems. The heading GERMAN POETRY--HISTORY AND CRITICISM is for a book that contains essays about German poetry.

Genre headings such as SHORT STORIES or DRAMA are usually assigned only to items that contain many works of that genre. If a book contains just one story, and there are such books, it is not customary to make a genre added entry, although that would be a logical thing to do if one were interested in the retrieval of works of that genre. In the age of the card catalog it simply was not feasible. This improvement can be achieved more readily by the use of a computer, where available.

Since the number of genre headings is small as compared to the vast body of subject headings, it is feasible to make up one's own system. Terms used should be recorded in a list. Similar terms not used should be tied into this list with cross-references, as in the following example:

DRAMA
ESSAYS
PLAYS see DRAMA
SHORT STORIES

In many libraries literature headings must be subdivided by nationality. Most published lists confuse the concepts of nationality and language. AMERICAN DRAMA, for example, usually means plays written by Americans, i.e. residents of the United States of America. But SPANISH

DRAMA can mean plays written by Spaniards, by South Americans, or even plays written in or translated into Spanish. If possible, be consistent. Let American, English, Spanish, Mexican, etc. be ethnic adjectives when they modify genres. Use parenthetical qualifiers to indicate language, but only if necessary:

SWISS DRAMA (FRENCH)

But

MEXICAN DRAMA

Catalogers making their own list of genre headings should also be consistent in respect to typography. Let it be either

AMERICAN POETRY
AMERICAN ESSAYS
AMERICAN SHORT STORIES

or inverted

POETRY, AMERICAN
ESSAYS, AMERICAN
SHORT STORIES, AMERICAN

Of course, when a published list is used consistency may be unattainable. The prestigious *Library of Congress Subject Headings*, for example, mixes straight and inverted forms, giving AMERICAN POETRY, but SHORT STORIES, AMERICAN.

Ambiguity

To avoid ambiguity one must see to it that each categorical heading serves only one function. As we have noted, in the *Sears List of Subject Headings* the term SHORT STORY (singular) stands for the topic, while SHORT STORIES (plural) stands for the genre, for collections of short stories. Ideally, no one term should be made to serve both purposes. Unfortunately, a published list like the *Sears List of Subject Headings* may well furnish an ambiguous term like PIANO MUSIC.

This could designate a subject (a book about piano music) or a genre (an actual piece of music written for the piano). The leaves the cataloger with a choice: accept the "authorized" term and let the reader deal with the ambiguity, or assume responsibility and straighten out the conflict. The latter course would appear to be the more professional approach. This could be fairly simply done by the use of parenthetical qualifiers, such as

PIANO MUSIC (TOPIC)

versus

PIANO MUSIC (GENRE)

To sum up: a genre heading answers the question: Does this publication contain works of a certain kind?

FORMAT ADDED ENTRIES

Format added entries are for books that can be said to be of a certain format. They differ from genre added entries as well as from subject added entries. An example is shown in Figure 45.

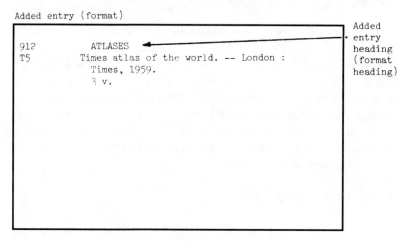

Added entry (format)

```
912        ATLASES  ◄─────────────────────
T5         Times atlas of the world. -- London :
           Times, 1959.
           3 v.
```

Added entry (format heading)

Figure 45. *A format added entry card*

The book thus cataloged is not a book about atlases, the way another book may be about sculpture. Nor can we say that it contains atlases, the way another book may contain short stories. Instead the entire book is in the format of an atlas. A heading of this kind helps readers find all atlases the library may have. Just as subject and genre headings must be controlled, format headings also must be taken from a published or homemade list that refers the user from terms not used to those that are used. Here is an example from a homemade list of format headings:

DICTIONARIES--FOREIGN LANGUAGE
LABORATORY MANUALS
UNABRIDGED DICTIONARIES see DICTIONARIES--ENGLISH
    LANGUAGE

The cross-reference UNABRIDGED DICTIONARIES see DICTIO-NARIES--ENGLISH LANGUAGE reminds the cataloger that no heading exists in the system for unabridged dictionaries and guides library users to the correct heading.

Published lists of subject headings, of course, contain many format headings. However, they are never marked as such and are intermingled with true subject headings. One has to be very watchful.

To sum up: a format heading answers the question: Is this publication of a certain format?

TRACINGS

As in the case of author and title added entries, all categorical headings, subject, genre, and format alike, must be traced at the foot of the corresponding main entries. Categorical tracings are traditionally numbered with Arabic numerals and precede all other tracings. Categorical tracings repeat the information contained in the heading and are typed in all capitals. Here is the tracing for the heading given to the chemistry book at the beginning of this chapter:

1. CHEMISTRY, ORGANIC

The tracings for genre and format headings are constructed in the same way:

1. SHORT STORIES
2. ATLASES

Unless the function of the categorical heading is indicated by parenthetical qualifiers, as in PIANO MUSIC (TOPIC), the distinction between subject, genre, and format is not indicated in the tracings.

Chapter Ten

Linked Entries or Analytics

Occasionally it is necessary to make catalog entries that show the relationships between works, documents, and items. Such linked added entries are often called "analytics." Analytics can be made for works contained with other works in a given publication, such as a play in an anthology. We refer to these here as work analytics. They can also be made for whole documents, i.e., books that form part of a set of books. We have called these document analytics.

WORK ANALYTICS

Many items, such as collections or anthologies, contain more than one work. A compact disc, for example, may contain several works of music. Work analytics, often just called analytics, can be made for them. Figure 46 shows an example of an analytic, carrying the work title in the added entry heading. Many a library patron will look for the same work under the composer's name. For that reason it will be a good idea to make an author/title analytic, as shown in Figure 47.

Tracings for Work Analytics

Like all other added entries, analytics must be traced at the foot of the main entry. Tracings for author and title added entries, including analytics, marked by Roman numerals. We add the abbreviation ATAN to indicate an author/title analytic, and TAN for a title analytic. The

```
PHONO       Holberg Suite, in
388         Peer Gynt suite, No.1 [and other
              music] / [by] Grieg. -- New York :
              Vincent, 1995.

            sound disc : digital ; 4 3/4 in.

            Vincent V991
```

Figure 46. *A title work analytic*

```
            Grieg, Edvard Hagerup
PHONO           Holberg Suite, in
388         Peer Gynt suite, No.1 [and other
              music] / [by] Grieg. -- New York :
              Vincent, 1995.

            sound disc : digital ; 4 3/4 in.

            Vincent V991
```

Figure 47. *An author/title work analytic*

tracings for the Peer Gynt example are shown in Figure 48. The analytics tracings, it should be noted, repeat the information that is given in the heading, including the word "in."

```
PHONO
388         Peer Gynt suite, No.1 [and other
            music] / [by] Grieg. -- New York :
            Vincent, 1995.

            sound disc : digital ; 4 3/4 in.

            Vincent V991


I. Grieg, Edvard Hagerup. II. ATAN: Grieg, Edvard
Hagerup: Holberg Suite, in III. TAN: Holberg Suite,
in
```

Figure 48. *Main entry with tracings*

DOCUMENT ANALYTICS (SET PRINCIPLE)

Some multi-volume sets are cataloged as a unit (i.e., under the set description principle, main entry made for the set) as illustrated in Figure 49.

```
N
90          Essays on contemporary art / edited
E8          by Joe Doe. -- Milano : Eta, 1984
            2 v.


            Contents: v.1. American art today --
            v.2. The European art scene




1. ART, MODERN. I. Doe, Joe, ed.  TAN
```

Figure 49. *Main entry showing contents, with simplified tracings*

```
N           American art today, v.1 of
90          Essays on contemporary art / edited
E8          by Joe Doe. -- Milano : Eta, 1984
            2 v.
```

Figure 50. *Document analytic*

Since the two document or volume titles are given in the contents note
the tracings for the analytics can be simplified. The entire set would be
found under "Essays." The first volume would be found under "American" by means of the document analytic illustrated in Figure 50.

DOCUMENT ANALYTICS (DOCUMENT PRINCIPLE)

Sometimes the individual books in a set are cataloged separately (i.e.,
under the document description principle). In that case there is no
main entry for the set. Yet it may be necessary to connect the document main entries to the title of their parent set. Consider a set of two
books by Richard Blum, entitled *Drugs*. Volume 1 is entitled *Society
and Drugs* and volume 2 is entitled *Students and Drugs*. The two volumes, dealing with slightly different aspects of the problem, were
catalogued separately, one main entry each. Since the set was split up
there is, of course, no main entry for the set as a whole. For the person who might be looking for Blum's *Drugs* it would therefore be advisable to make added entries to connect the volumes to the set. Such
"connective" added entries, as shown in Figures 51 and 52, would tie
these three titles together.

```
             Drugs, v.1
  616
  S7       Society and drugs / Richard H.
           Blum. -- San Francisco : Jossey-
           Bass, 1974.

           376 p.

           (Drugs, v.1)
```

Figure 51. *A connective added entry*

```
             Drugs, v.2
  616
  S7       Society and drugs / Richard H.
           Blum. -- San Francisco : Jossey-
           Bass, 1974.

           376 p.

           (Drugs, v.2)
```

Figure 52. *A second connective added entry*

Now users can look under "Society," under "Students," or under "Drugs": they will find these books either way, which is better access than most large libraries can offer.

Tracings for Connectives

Connective added entries are a form of title added entries. They can be traced as shown in Figure 53 and 54 (we propose the abbreviation TCON to indicate the type of added entry).

```
616
S7        Society and drugs / Richard H.
             Blum. - San Francisco : Jossey-
             Bass, 1974.

          376 p.

          (Drugs, v.1)


1. DRUG ABUSE.  I. Blum, Richard H.
II. TCON: Drugs, v.1
```

Figure 53. *Tracings for a connective added entry*

```
362.2
S8        Students and drugs / Richard H.
             Blum. -- San Francisco : Jossey-
             Bass, 1974.

          380 p.

          (Drugs, v.2)


1. CHILDREN--DRUG USE. 2. DRUG ABUSE--YOUTH.
3. TEENAGERS--DRUG ABUSE. I. Blum, Richard H.
II. TCON: Drugs, v.2
```

Figure 54. *Tracings for a connective added entry*

SUBJECT ANALYTICS

Occasionally it may be necessary to indicate the subject of a work for which an analytic is made. Figure 55 shows an example which has been done by a subject/title analytic. This analytic tells the reader that important material on White Dwarfs is found in volume 3 of this ten-volume set. To show the tracings, the corresponding main entry record is shown in Figure 56. The abbreviation SAN stands for subject analytic.

Occasionally a work contains noteworthy chapters that need to be brought to readers' attention. A book on astronomy, for example, may have a chapter on Red Giants. A chapter analytic might be helpful, as shown in Figure 57. The corresponding main entry with tracings might look like the card shown in Figure 58.

The labor of designing, typing, tracing, and filing analytics is considerable. That is why they are not often made. In addition to those shown here, other methods of making analytics could be devised. Whatever style a library adopts for its analytics, however, the cataloger must see to it that some sort of tracing is made on the main entry so that no "blind" entries are left in the catalog should the item ever be withdrawn.

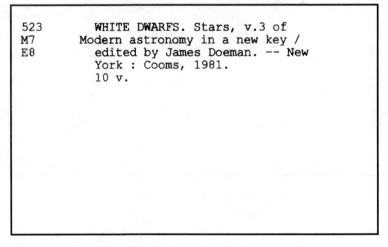

```
523        WHITE DWARFS. Stars, v.3 of
M7         Modern astronomy in a new key /
E8             edited by James Doeman. -- New
           York : Cooms, 1981.
           10 v.
```

Figure 55. *A subject/title added entry card*

```
523
M7        Modern astronomy in a new key /
E8           edited by James Doeman. -- New
          York : Cooms, 1981.
          10 v.




1. ASTRONOMY. 2. SAN: WHITE DWARFS. Stars,
v.3 of I. Doeman, James, ed.
```

Figure 56. *Tracings for a subject analytic*

```
523        RED GIANTS, ch.8 of
W7         World of stars / [by] Frank Unger. --
           New York : Scipress, 2000.

           560 p.
```

Figure 57. *A subject analytic*

```
523
W7        World of stars / [by] Frank Unger. --
          New York : Scipress, 2000.

          560 p.




1. STARS. 2. SAN: RED GIANTS, ch.8 of
I. Unger, Frank.
```

Figure 58. *Main entry with tracings for an analytic*

Chapter Eleven

Shelf List

Most added entries are made for the public. They can be called public added entries and are filed in the public catalog. But some added entries serve the housekeeping purposes of the library. They are kept in the librarian's workroom where they are filed by location code in the same order as the books on the shelf, whence the name "shelf list" for this part of the catalog.

While public added entries are made selectively as needed (or not at all if thought unnecessary), a shelf list entry is made for every main entry record in the catalog, without exception. The shelf list, therefore, is the librarian's complete record not only of what is on the shelf but of all that belongs there.

The shelf list is divided into as many sections as there are different files in the library. A library that has materials in the following three files

Book stacks
Reference books
Indexes

will have a shelf list in three sections: stack shelf list, reference shelf list, and indexes shelf list. Within each section the cards are arranged by location codes, by accession number, by title, or however else the materials are arranged on the shelf.

```
E
184         Chinatown, U. S. A. / by Calvin
C5            Lee. -- Garden Grove, NH :
              Doubleton, 1965.
              154 p.


gift of Dr. Marcia Blain
lost Dec 75
c.2 Mar 76
```

Figure 59. *A shelf list card*

TYPOGRAPHY

The shelf list card looks very much like the main entry. It contains the same location code, bibliographic description, and physical description as the main entry. Notes and tracings are omitted to gain space for housekeeping information such as a record of copies in the collection, losses, replacements, whether gift or purchase, date of acquisition, etc. Figure 59 shows an example of a shelf list card.

The housekeeping information recorded on this shelf list card reveals that the first copy was lost and later replaced. The library now owns one copy of this book, copy 2. If in April 2000 another copy of the same book is acquired, it receives the same location code to which will be added the copy designation "c. 3" since it is the third copy the library has owned. On the shelf list card this information is recorded: c. 3 Apr 2000. Notice that copy numbers are used only once. If copy 1 is lost or discarded, no other copy of that book will ever be called c. 1 again.

PERIODICALS RECORDS

For the holdings of periodicals and other subscriptions a different kind of housekeeping system is often used. Periodicals are usually weeklies

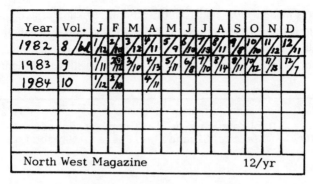

Figure 60. *A periodical record card*

or monthlies. As each issue is received by the library the date of receipt is entered onto a periodical record card. This is more efficient than constant removal and handling of the shelf list card. Figure 60 shows a typical periodical record card.

Such cards in many designs are available from library supply houses. Many are constructed so that they can be filed flat in shingled trays in so-called visible file or indexing cabinets. This simplifies consultation of the list because all one has to do is to flip up the next card to gain access to the desired one. No removal and replacement of cards is necessary.

The example in Figure 60 shows that the issue for March 1984 failed to arrive and had to be claimed. It also shows that the issue for February of 1983 was lost and that vol. 8 was bound.

FILE SPLITTERS

Occasionally, a library owns two or more copies of a book. When one of these copies resides in one file (say, the reference shelves) and the others elsewhere (say, the regular stacks) a problem arises at the shelf list. For in the public catalog all copies are represented by one main entry, and consequently only one shelf list card is made. Yet one cannot file one card in two places in the shelf list. The dilemma is solved by splitting the shelf list record. One of the files is designated as the home file (say, the reference shelves). The shelf list card is filed in the reference shelf list. The other file is called the alternate file. A dummy shelf

list card is made for the stack shelf list. Figure 61 shows the main entry
for a file splitter. In the reference shelf list (the home file shelf list) a
shelf list card is placed, as shown in Figure 62. In the stack shelf list,
the alternate file shelf list, a dummy is placed, as shown in Figure 63.

```
REF
PC         Dictionnaire de la langue francaise /
2540          Jerome Livage. -- Paris : Hautcourt,
L5            1925.



another copy stacks



1. FRENCH LANGUAGE--DICTIONARIES. I. Livage,
Jerome
```

Figure 61. *A main entry pointing to two files*

```
REF
PC         Dictionnaire de la langue francaise /
2540          Jerome Livage. -- Paris : Hautcourt,
L5             1925.



c.1
c.2 stacks
```

Figure 62. *A home file shelf list card*

```
                                        dummy SL

    PC        Dictionnaire de la langue francaise /
    2540          Jerome Livage. -- Paris : Hautcourt,
    L5            1925.


                        for full information
                        see  REF
                             PC
                             2540
                             L5



    c.2
```

Figure 63. *An alternate file shelf list card*

Now the housekeeping records are complete and clear. While the title was cataloged only once, every copy of the book is represented by its shelf list card.

FILE STRADDLERS

When the parts of a series straddle two or more files, a similar procedure will keep the shelf list records organized. Figure 64 shows the main entry for such a set. Figure 65 shows the shelf list card for the home file. A dummy shelf list card is made for the alternate file, as shown in Figure 66.

If a file splitter or straddler is ever removed from the library's holdings, it goes without saying that all shelf list cards must be removed, including the dummies. If that step is forgotten a blind reference is left in the shelf list.

A note on tracings: Since shelf list entries are mandatory, it is not necessary to leave any tracings on the main entry. Only public added entries are traced.

```
REF
JC          Freedom of speech : an annual survey /
591            Louisville, KY : Freedom Press, 1993-
F8




Latest REF
Older years STACKS
```

Figure 64. *A main entry pointing to two files*

```
REF
JC          Freedom of speech : an annual survey /
591            Louisville, KY : Freedom Press, 1993-
F8



2000
1993- 1999 STACKS
```

Figure 65. *A home file shelf list card*

```
                                    dummy SL
JC          Freedom of speech : an annual survey /
591            Louisville, KY : Freedom Press, 1993-
F8




1993- 1999
```

Figure 66. *An alternate file shelf list card*

Chapter Twelve

Cross-References

Even the most experienced library worker cannot remember all the headings under which relevant entries are filed in the catalog. Not even a veteran cataloger can memorize all the decisions that have been made in the past concerning the forms of names and headings used or not used. To keep the catalog at its highest level of usefulness for users and librarians alike, a coherent system of cross-references is maintained.

Cross-references are of two kinds. There are special references from and to clearly defined terms, and there are general references to classes of terms not specifically detailed.

Special cross-references are further divided into two distinctly different types. A cross-reference either refers the library user from a term not used in the catalog to one used. This is the *See* reference. Or they go from a term used in the catalog to one or more terms that are also used, which is the so-called *See also* reference.

The words *see* and *see also* are commonly underlined (or printed in italics) to indicate that they are not part of the cross-referenced terms.

SEE REFERENCES

See references are used to guide library users to alternate forms of author's names and to alternate categorical headings. They can be made from any unused term the cataloger chooses to the appropriate term that is used as a heading in the catalog. Most subject *See* references, however, will be made at the suggestion of the published list of headings that has been adopted. In the *Sears List of Subject Headings* such suggestions take this form: Names, Fictitious *See* Pseudonyms. Figures 67 and 68 show some examples: two author cross-references, laid out in block format for easier typing.

```
Clemens, Samuel Langhorne
see
Twain, Mark
```

```
Lawick-Goodall, Jane, Barones van
see
Van Lawick-Goodall, Jane
```

Figure 67. *Two author cross-reference cards*

```
NEGRO HISTORY
see
AFRO-AMERICANS--HISTORY
```

```
PORTER, WILLIAM SIDNEY
see
HENRY, O.
```

Figure 68. *Two subject cross-reference cards*

The INSPEC Thesaurus and many other similar specialized lists of headings employ USE references instead of see references, like this example: Diesel engines USE Internal combustion engines. For the card catalog this suggestion translates into

DIESEL ENGINES
see
INTERNAL COMBUSTION ENGINES

The *See* reference takes the reader from one heading to one equivalent or approximately equivalent heading. Logically, then, the *See* reference is a 1:1 (one-to-one) reference. It is a reference that leads from one term (Clemens, Samuel Langhorne) to one other term (Twain, Mark). Catalogers who follow established lists of subject headings will occasionally find this logic defeated. In the *Sears List*, for example, many of the suggested *See* references lead to more than one term. An example is the following:

Welfare state. *See* Economic policy; Public welfare; State, The

It is not clear from such a reference to which term one should turn. Is "Economic policy" the equivalent of "Welfare state"? Or is it part of the problem, or maybe the solution? It would be clearer if the 1:1 principle were adhered to, A See B, followed as necessary by B *see also* C, D, etc. Figure 69 shows the "Welfare state" example restructured. This gives

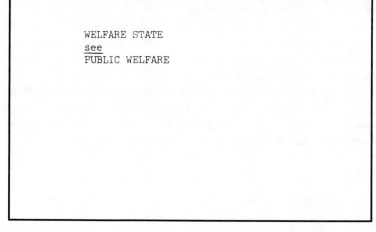

Figure 69. *A subject cross-reference card for Welfare state*

```
PUBLIC WELFARE
see also
ECONOMIC POLICY
```

Figure 70. *A subject cross-reference card for Public welfare*

the catalog user a precise instruction where to look. Under Public welfare, Economic policy can be mentioned in a *see also* reference, as shown in Figure 70.

Under Economic policy, finally, other references might lead to relevant terms such as ECONOMIC ASSISTANCE or SOCIAL POLICY.

SEE ALSO REFERENCES

See also references are used to guide library users from a heading that is in use to one or more other headings that are also in use and may be helpful. *See also* references are made as needed at the suggestion of the published list of headings adopted. The *Sears List*, in an example shown in Chapter 9, suggested: Tombs *See also* Brasses; Catacombs; Cemeteries; etc. If the library has one or more books under the heading TOMBS, one or more others under the heading CEMETERIES, but nothing under the headings BRASSES or CATACOMBS, then the cataloger will make one of the suggested cross-references:

TOMBS
see also
CEMETERIES

Obviously, *see also* references do not attempt to guide readers to equivalent headings, only to related ones. consequently, *see also* references can lead from a wider term to a narrower one or from a narrower term to a wider one, or they can connect terms that are on the same level of extension.

In specialized lists of terms, such as *INSPEC Thesaurus*, cross-reference directions often replace *see also* with abbreviations, such as BT for "broader term," RT for "related term," and so on: Internal combustion engines BT Engines RT Ignition. In the card catalog this translates to

INTERNAL COMBUSTION ENGINES
see also
ENGINES
IGNITION

assuming, of course, that the library has material under all three headings. A case could be made for making such references even if nothing was under INTERNAL COMBUSTION ENGINES, on the theory that a see also reference is better than nothing.

Figures 71, 72, and 73 are examples of a few other *see also* references. This one goes from a general to a specific heading, which is the most common direction. The next one goes from a narrow, specific term

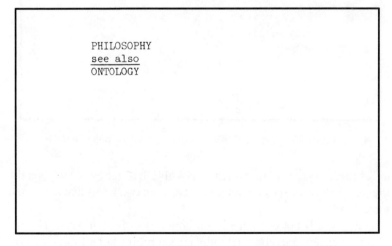

```
PHILOSOPHY
see also
ONTOLOGY
```

Figure 71. *A subject cross-reference card for Philosophy*

```
      VACUUM TUBES
      see also
      ELECTRONICS
```

Figure 72. *A subject cross-reference card for Vacuum tubes*

```
      TROUBADOURS
      see also
      TROUVERES
```

Figure 73. *A subject cross-reference card for Troubadours*

to a broad, general term, which is possible but not common. Finally, Figure 73 shows a *see also* reference between two terms that are on the same level.

The reader is not compelled to follow a *see also* reference. The *see also* reference is merely a helpful suggestion. It can be from one term used in the catalog to one or more terms also used. This last condition, also used, is essential because nothing is more annoying than a reference to a term that is not there.

GENERAL REFERENCES

Occasionally, general references are made. They use any suitable free text instead of the formalized *see also* structure. Figure 74 is an example. An overview of the various types of cross-references that occur in library catalogs is shown in Table 2.

```
ABORTION

For pamphlets, brochures, and
similar uncataloged material
on this topic consult the
pamphlet file
```

Figure 74. *A general reference card*

Table 2 Types of cross references

Special cross references	General cross reference
see	to a certain file
1:1, from a term not used to an equivalent term used	to a class of terms
see also	general message
1:1, from a term used to another term used	
1:many, from a term used to two or more terms also used	

CONTROLS

Whenever the term to which a cross-reference refers is withdrawn from the catalog, the cross-reference must also be withdrawn or a blind reference will be left in the catalog. Unfortunately, no cataloger can remember all the cross-references that are made. The librarian must therefore rely on a control system as a memory aid. In the case of subject references, the kind that is used most frequently, such a control system can be in the form of notes penciled right into the list of subject headings adopted by the library. Some libraries use lists that leave every other column blank for just this purpose. Here is a see reference from the *Sears List*:

Toadstools see Mushrooms

Here is the *Sears List* entry for Mushrooms:

Mushrooms 589.2
See also Fungi
x Toadstools
xx Fungi

The line marked "x" is a "control." The symbol "x" means that a *see* reference was made from Toadstools to Mushrooms. If the library has books under MUSHROOMS, the cataloger might follow the suggestion and add the following cross-reference to the catalog, as shown in Figure 75.

If that is done, then some control marking should be made in the *Sears List*, in pencil for easier erasing:

Mushrooms 589.2
See also Fungi
x Toadstools **
xx Fungi

A similar mark should be made next to the cross-reference that points in the opposite direction and is printed under T in the same list:

**Toadstools *See* Mushrooms

```
TOADSTOOLS
see
MUSHROOMS
```

Figure 75. *A subject cross-reference card*

If it should happen later that the last book on mushrooms is withdrawn, a blind reference would be left. To prevent that, the cataloger, on withdrawing the last card with the subject heading MUSHROOMS, looks up the term "Mushrooms" in the *Sears List* and finds that the line "x Toadstools" has been marked. This reminds the cataloger to go back to the catalog and pull the cross-reference from Toadstools to Mushrooms. All that remains to be done now is to erase the control marks in the book under Mushrooms and under Toadstools.

Of course, the moment a new edition of the *Sears List* is published and adopted by the library all those penciled control marks are lost unless they are faithfully transferred to the new book, a tedious job subject to human error. An alternate way to control cross-references is to maintain a control file on cards.

A simple control file can be designed as follows. Any cross-reference goes *from* something *to* something. On a cross-reference card, the card that is filed in the public catalog, the term on top can be called the FROM term. The term below is the TO term. A control card, then, is the obverse of the cross-reference card: it shows the TO term on top and the FROM term below. The FROM term is marked with the already familiar symbols that indicate type of reference (x = *see* from; xx = *see also* from). Figure 76 shows a cross-reference with its control card. The control card tells the cataloger that a see also reference was made from

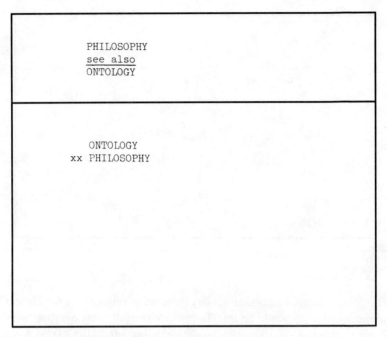

Figure 76. *A cross-reference and corresponding control card*

PHILOSOPHY to ONTOLOGY. The control card for the Mark Twain reference is shown in Figure 77. It tells the cataloger that a *see* reference was made from Clemens to Twain.

While the cross-reference cards in the public catalog are filed by the FROM term, the control cards are filed by the TO term in the same place where the shelf list is kept. Should it happen that a cross-reference goes from one term to several terms, such as in the Figure 78, then separate control cards are made for each TO term, as shown in Figure 79.

What would happen if the term PROJECTION were abolished? The removed heading is checked against the control file. The control card shown above reminds the cataloguer that a *see also* reference exists from PERSPECTIVE to PROJECTION. No one could possibly have remembered this without the aid of the control file. The term PROJECTION on the cross-reference card is now crossed out and the PROJEC-

```
     Twain, Mark
   x Clemens, Samuel Langhorne
```

Figure 77. *A control card*

```
   PERSPECTIVE
   see also
   DRAWING
   PROJECTION
```

Figure 78. *A subject cross-reference card*

TION control card is removed from the control file. Figure 80 shows what is left in the public catalog. Figure 81 shows the card that remains in the control file.

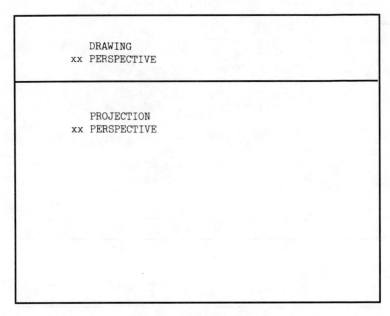

Figure 79. *Two control cards*

In the
public
catalog

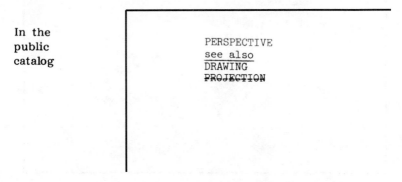

Figure 80. *An amended cross-reference card*

Important: blind references may result if the control file is not checked each time the last card for a heading is removed from the catalog.

Occasionally, general references have to be inserted into the catalog to guide readers. There is no standard format for general references. Libraries use them in two ways. One kind consists of a few explanatory

In the control file

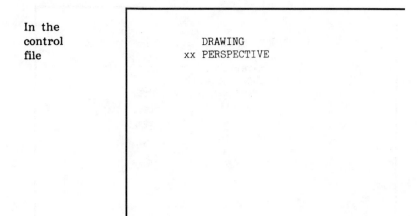

```
                DRAWING
            xx PERSPECTIVE
```

Figure 81. *A control card*

words guiding readers from a term to a certain special file of materials. The general reference for ABORTION (Figure 74) is one example. Such general references need not be controlled. Instead, when the last pamphlet on abortion is discarded, the public catalog is checked. The general reference filed under ABORTION is simply removed from the catalog.

Sometimes general references are used to guide readers from one term to a whole class of others. An example is shown in Figure 82. The control card for this general reference looks like the card shown in Figure 83.

If the subject heading MUSIC--QUOTATIONS, MAXIMS, ETC. is removed from the catalog, the control file will warn the cataloger to either remove the general reference from the catalog or to change the example on it.

One thing that often mystifies library personnel long after they think they have understood the mechanism of cross-references and controls is the distinction between "see also" and "xx." The explanation, therefore, bears repeating. If any published list of subject headings shows an entry like this:

Tornadoes
See also Cyclones; Storms
xx Storms; Winds

```
        QUOTATIONS, MAXIMS, ETC.

        Relevant material may be found under
        certain subjects, e.g.
        MUSIC--QUOTATIONS, MAXIMS, ETC.
```

Figure 82. *A general reference card*

```
             MUSIC--QUOTATIONS, MAXIMS, ETC.
        gen. QUOTATIONS, MAXIMS, ETC.
```

Figure 83. *A control card for a general reference*

this means that three see also references are suggested. They are shown in Figure 84. The reader should notice that no references are suggested from Tornadoes to Winds and from Cyclones to Tornadoes.

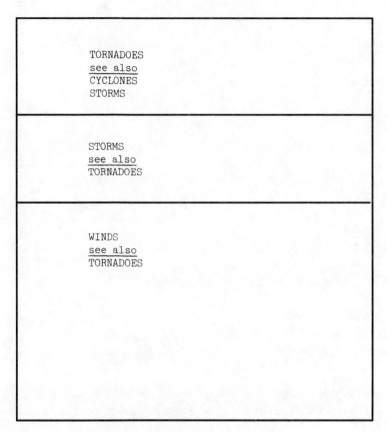

Figure 84. *Three see also references*

Chapter Thirteen

Filing

For the card catalog to be useful, the entries in it must be arranged in a systematic way. It is often said that catalog cards are filed alphabetically. This is an oversimplification. In reality there are three different ordering principles that apply from case to case. Certainly, many entries are filed alphabetically:

Some selected
Two for tea
Under elm trees

in other words, S, T, U. But others are filed numerically:

3 Musketeers . . .
4 in a . . .
5 famous plays . . .

And some are filed by context:

Athenaeum of Philadelphia
Guide to museum . . .
ATHENAEUM OF PHILADELPHIA
Beginnings of the American . . .

i.e., the corporate author before the subject of the same name, regardless of the alphabetical order of the words that follow.

The basic principle underlying all three examples is that a correctly filed entry follows an entry of lower rank and is followed by an entry of higher rank. How to determine the rank of entries has been codified in a book, *ALA Filing Rules* (American Library Association, Chicago, 1980). These guidelines are widely accepted as standard in American libraries. They are followed here in principle with minor changes.

In the past, it was often said that filing meant putting "words" in order. ALA Filing Rules recognize a broader concept, replacing "word" by what is known as "character string."

A character is any graphic symbol used as a unit in writing or printing. The letter A, for example, is an alphabetical character. The numeral 3 is a numeric character. The sign $ is another type of character. Any single character, and any group of two or more characters that stand together, forms a character string. Thus, a word is a character string. But notice: not all character strings are words.

There are two kinds of character strings: alphabetic strings and numeric strings.

ALPHABETIC FILING

An alphabetic character string can be defined as a letter or group of letters or other nonnumeric characters set off by numeric characters, spaces, dashes, hyphens, diagonal slashes, or periods (the six alphabetic string delimiters). Here are some examples of alphabetic character strings:

BIOLOGY

This is a purely alphabetic string, seven alphabetic characters surrounded by spaces.

ART--HISTORY

Both of these strings are delimited by a space on one side and a dash on the other. Since the typewriter does not have a dash two hyphens are customarily used to simulate it.

Lloyd-Jones

These two strings are delimited by a space on one side and a hyphen on the other.

and/or

These are two strings because they have a space on one side and a diagonal slash on the other.

Selected works.

The word "works" is a string because it starts with a space and ends with a period.

Boy's

This is one alphabetic character string, too. It consists of four letters and one non-numeric character set off by spaces. Notice that the apostrophe is not a string delimiter but is a symbol that is ignored, where "ignored" means that it is treated as if it were not there, not as if it were a space. For filing purposes, thus, the following three strings are equivalent: boys, boy's, and boys'.

3M

Here the letter M is one character string. It is delimited on the left by the numeric character 3 and on the right by a space. By the same token, 3 is a numeric string, but more about numeric strings below.

Alphabetic strings are filed in the customary order of the English alphabet. In reality, of course, so-called alphabetical filing is nothing but a special case of numerical filing. For when we arrange the letters of the English alphabet in their alphabetical order we actually map them mentally, one for one, to the sequence of integers from +1 to +26. Here is a table that shows how we map them:

A 1	H 8	O 15	U 21
B 2	I 9	P 16	V 22
C 3	J 10	Q 17	W 23
D 4	K 11	R 18	X 24
E 5	L 12	S 19	Y 25
F 6	M 13	T 20	Z 26
G 7	N 14		

After mapping the letters to their numerical equivalents we can put them in rank order. Thus, when we file B behind A we do so because

B = 2, A = 1, and 1 is less than 2. In other words, we file B behind A because B outranks A, has a higher numerical value.

Often two compared alphabetic strings begin with different letters. Rank order is then determined on the basis of the difference in the first letter (Abel is less than Baker).

Sometimes strings begin with the same letters. The rank difference is then determined by a subsequent letter pair. Here is an example:

Abel
Abraham

The difference here comes in the third letter pair, e vs. r. Since e = 5, r = 18, and 5 is less than 18, we file Abel before Abraham. Occasionally two compared strings correspond in symbol content to the very end of one of them. Here is an example:

Abel
Abelson

Rank difference here comes in the fifth letter pair. After the fourth letter in "Abel" is "nothing. " After the fourth letter in "Abelson" is "s." "Nothing," of course, is mapped to the number 0; "s," to 19. And since 0 is less than 19, Abelson outranks Abel. In the ALA Filing Rules the phenomenon of the zero-valued space is given the picturesque name of the "nothing before something" rule.

Often two compared entries begin with the same string. Filing then proceeds by the next string as in this example:

Mass media in . . .
Mass violence in . . .

It is important to note that library filing is string by string:

Beaver dam
Beaver Falls
Beaverbrook

and not character by character as, for example, in *Collier's Encyclopedia*:

Beaverbrook
Beaver dam
Beaver Falls

Different persons occasionally have identical names. Filing then is by given names:

Frederick, John
Frederick, Justus

Occasionally, two persons have exactly the same name. Filing is then by date:

Vianna, Oduvaldo, 1892-1972
Vianna, Oduvaldo, 1936-1974

As the catalog grows in size, different books by the same author will appear. Since in such cases the author headings are identical, filing proceeds by the title:

Frost, Robert
Boy's will ...
Frost, Robert
In the clearing ...

The same thing happens when two books are cataloged under identical subject headings:

TEACHING
Humanism in the ...
TEACHING
Retreat from learning ...

One important principle of the ALA Filing Rules is that alphabetic characters are considered in exactly the form and order in which they appear in the string. This principle emphasizes how character strings look rather than how they sound or what they mean.

The following sections review some of the fine points of alphabetic filing (the rule numbers refer to the ALA Filing Rules of 1980).

Mc vs. Mac (Rules 1 and 2.1)

Filers familiar with the old ALA rules of 1968 remember that McFarland was filed as if it were spelled MacFarland. This is no longer done. All alphabetic strings are filed as spelled, not as pronounced. Thus, the following three words are in correct order:

MacGower
Machinery
McFarland

Modified Letters (Rule 1.1)

Modified letters are treated like their unmodified counterparts. The German ä is considered equivalent to the English a. The Spanish ñ is equated with the simple n. Also, the ligature œ is considered to be equal to the letter o followed by the letter e; the Spanish digraph ll is considered to be an l followed by another l, and so forth. The following names are in correct order:

Oberg
Öster
Østerling
Ostrowsky
Ulloa
Ulmer

Note that some libraries will file the German ä as if spelled ae, ö as if spelled oe, and so on. Spanish librarians will file the digraph ll after the plain l.

Letters of non-Latin alphabets such as Greek ψ becomes psi. The component letters are then mapped to 16, 19, and 9, respectively. After this, the Greek letter can be filed:

Partnership
ψ factor (i.e., Psi factor)
Psychology

Non-alphabetic Non-numeric Signs and Symbols (Rule 1. 2)

In alphabetic strings all non-alphabetic symbols that are neither numeric symbols nor other string delimiters (i.e., not dash, hyphen, slash, or period) are ignored, where ignored means treated as if they did not exist, not as if they were spaces. Thus K*A*P*L*A*N is filed as KAPLAN. Warning: letters, signs, and symbols in numeric strings follow different rules.

Numeric Symbols Next to Alphabetic Characters (Rule 8. 6)

If a numeric symbol stands next to an alphabetic string, it is considered a string delimiter and is not considered to be part of the adjacent alphabetic string. The following three lines are in correct order:

H2O (i.e., the alphabetic string H followed by the
numeric string 2)
H and H
Horvath

It should be noted that, all else being equal, numbers file before letters, "H 2" before "H and."

AMPERSAND (RULE 1. 3)

The most practical way to deal with the ampersand sign (&) is probably the "with" option of Rule 1.3. Under that option, the symbol & is filed as if it were spelled out in the language in question. The following entries are in order:

A & O International (& = and, English)
A and P Company
A & B Internationale (& = et, French)
A un joven
A & O im Ganzen (& = und, German)
A une dame

Abbreviations (Rule 3)

Abbreviations that do not function as terms of honor and address (cf. Rule 10, below) are arranged exactly as written. Thus, "Mr." files as the string MR between "Misty" and "Muzhik," in other words not as if spelled Mister. The following data elements are in correct filing order:

Mississippi
Mister Roberts
Mr. Adams
Ms. Adams

Initial Articles (Rule 4)

This rule directs filers to ignore all leading articles in the nominative case. This is easy to do in English where there are only three such articles: a, an, and the. But the rule applies to all languages, which makes it hard for persons of limited linguistic background. For the cataloger, in order to follow the rule, must be careful to distinguish among cases, such as nominative, dative, and accusative, and between articles, numerals, and pronouns. Here are some examples:

The Black Hole *becomes* Black Hole
Ein Ding zum Lachen *becomes* Ding zum Lachen
Los jovenes de ayer *becomes* Jovenes de ayer

"The," "Ein," and "Los," are articles in the nominative case. But compare these examples

Ein Ding weiss ich gewiss
Los de Abajo

These two examples file under "Ein" and "Los," respectively, because "ein" is a numeral or possibly an article in the accusative case, and "Los" is a pronoun. Many catalogers and catalog users may find it too difficult to distinguish between articles and other types of words of this nature. A compromise is possible: drop all English initial articles (a, an, the) and leave all non-English words in place. Here are the same examples in compromise order:

Black Hole
Ein Ding weiss ich gewiss
Ein Ding zum Lachen
Los de Abajo
Los jovenes de ayer

Initial articles that are part of a proper name, such as the Los in Los Angeles, are treated as prefixes according to Rule 6. Articles that appear inside a title or heading, i.e., not in the initial or leading position, are filed like other strings:

Will a unicorn . . .
Will and power
Will the hustler
Will they conquer . . .
Williamsburg

Initials (Rule 5)

Initials are single letter abbreviations of words or names. They are treated as single letter strings:

Greasepaint
I am a camera
I. and his friend J.
I built a bridge
Iambic pentameters

Initialisms and Acronyms (Rule 5)

Initialisms, acronyms, and other abbreviations consisting of two or more characters enclosed by string delimiters (i.e., numerical characters, spaces, dashes, hyphens, slashes, and periods) are treated as alphabetic strings or "words":

I must go now
I.N.T.E.L.S.A.T. (I-space-N-space etc.)
Iberian Peninsula

IBM Applications Program
If this be error

Prefixes (Rule 6)

Prefixes in proper names that are separated from the rest of the name by a space or a hyphen are treated as separate strings. Prefixes connected with the name by an apostrophe are considered part of the name:

Damask
D'Arcy, John (i.e., DARCY)
De Forest, Angela
Death comes
Defoe
Lobo-Zarra, Arturo
Lobos
Los Angeles
Losable and lost

Double Names (Rule 3)

Double names such as "Watts-Dunton, Theodore" or "Lloyd George, David" are treated according to the regular rules for alphabetic strings:

Lloyd, Emma
Lloyd George, David
Lloyd, Sarah
Watts, Beulah
Watts-Dunton, Theodore
Watts, George M

Relators (Rule 9)

Abbreviations such as "ed." or "comp." following an author's name are called relators or function designators. They are disregarded in filing.

Terms of Honor (Rule 10)

Terms of honor and address added to names in author and subject headings, such as "Lord," "Sir," "Dr.," "Mr.," are disregarded:

John, Dr. Ambrose
John, Charles
John, Nancy
John, Mrs. William

NUMERIC FILING

Numeric strings have their own rules. A numeric string can be defined as any Arabic or Roman numeral or group of numeric characters, with or without punctuation marks and alphabetical auxiliaries that together express one cardinal or ordinal number. Here are ten numeric strings (not in any order):

5
V (Roman five)
5th
5e (French ordinal, equals 5th)
5. (German ordinal, equals 5th)
15
XV (Roman fifteen)
1/5 (a fraction, equals .2)
.2 (a decimal fraction, equals 1/5)
2 4/5 (a mixed number, equals 2.8)

According to Rule 1 all numeric strings file before alphabetic strings.

200 years
1001 nights
Abendstern
Best
The year 2000
The year after

When ranked among themselves, numeric strings, cardinal and ordinal numbers being treated alike, are filed in ascending numerical order (Rule 8).

Numerical strings placed next to non-numerical characters which do not have numerical significance are considered to be separated from these non-numerical characters:

2G Model 6 (filed as 2 G)
2^e partie (2^e, French equivalent of 2nd, is filed as 2)
200 Notions
200T Model . . .
200 Uncommon . . .

As shown in the example above, non-numerical characters which do have numerical significance in numerical strings are considered part of the numerical strings.

One fine point of numerical filing was left unsettled by the *ALA Filing Rules* of 1980, namely the rank order of fractions. It is recommended here that all fractions are filed by their numerical values. Here is a comprehensive example:

.5 and the . . .
1/2 by a . . . (.5 and ½ are equivalent)
2 4/5
3.1416
V and more
5e arrondissement
5 can be
5th column
5. Mann
15 and then
XV could go
17th Army
17^e Couronne
200
5,000.3 (i.e., 5 thousand and 3/10)
Abendstern
Borgman, Hans, 1903–
Borgman, Hans, 1941–

Numbers that appear inside a heading rather than at the beginning are
also subarranged numerically:

LOUIS II
LOUIS III
LOUIS IV, DUKE OF . . .
LOUIS IV, KING OF
MARINE BIOLOGY
Mental Health, 6th Conference
Mental Health, 7th Conference
Mental health and . . .

Ranges of dates with unequal starting points are arranged in ascending
numerical order by starting points:

GREAT BRITAIN--HISTORY--1660-1714
GREAT BRITAIN--HISTORY--1689-1714

Ranges of dates with identical starting points are arranged in ascending
numerical order by their endpoints:

GREAT BRITAIN--POLITICS AND GOVERNMENT--1485-1509
GREAT BRITAIN--POLITICS AND GOVERNMENT--1485-1603

If a single number or open range and a closed range with identical starting point are to be compared, the single number files first:

. . . HISTOR--1900-
. . . HISTORY--1900-1914

History headings of mixed alpha-numeric construction ought to be filed
in chronological order, not alphabetically:

. . . HISTORY--REVOLUTION, 1775-1783
. . . HISTORY--CIVIL WAR, 1861-1865

If numbers are spelled out they are filed alphabetically, not numerically:

Twenty years
Two men

CONTEXTUAL FILING

When two compared entries differ in access points, filing is based on simple alphabetical or numerical rank order. When two compared entries have equivalent headings, as in this example,

Nash, Ogden
Old dog barks . . .
Nash, Ogden
You can't get . . .

filing proceeds by the next element that is different, in this case "Old" before "You." In this case the headings were equal in symbol content as well as in function: they were both author headings. But occasionally it happens that two compared entries have headings that are equivalent in symbol content, but one is an author heading, the other is a subject heading:

Aristotle
Republic and other . . .
ARISTOTLE
Life of Aristotle . . .

Two entries of this kind are filed, not alphabetically (Life before Republic) but according to function or context (Aristotle as author before Aristotle as subject). Of course, when author and title entries are interfiled, the arrangement is straightforward and function is ignored:

Frost damage on citrus . . .
Frost in perspective
Frost, Robert
Selected works by . . .
Frost und sein Kreis . . .

Also, when different subject headings beginning with the same word are interfiled, arrangement is straightforward:

WASHINGTON CALENDAR
WASHINGTON, GEORGE
WASHINGTON POST

Undivided subject headings are filed before divided subject headings beginning with the same main heading:

JEWS
History of seven . . .
JEWS--BIOGRAPHY
Five masters of the . . .

SUBARRANGEMENT

If two or more items have the same title, the *ALA Filing Rules* specify subarrangement by date (Rule 2.3):

Business law / by Carl Hinze. -- New York: Globe, 1978.
Business law / by Joe Doe. -- Chicago: Hopner, 1980.
Business law / by Carl Hinze. -- 2nd ed. -- New York : Globe, 1981.

The same rule applies when two compared subject entries have identical headings and identical titles:

PHILOSOPHY
What is philosophy? / by Marie White. -- New York: Domby, 1970.
PHILOSOPHY
What is philosophy? / by John Brown. -- Boston: Harms, 1980.

It may be easier for most readers if such entries are subarranged alphabetically by authors' last names:

Business law / by Joe Doe . . .
Business law / by Carl Hinze . . . 1978.
Business law / by Carl Hinze . . . 1981.
PHILOSOPHY
What is philosophy? / John Brown . . .
PHILOSOPHY
What is philosophy? / by Marie White . . .

Some titles consist of only one part, the "title proper." Filing of simple "titles proper" is straightforward:

Algebra / by Joe Doe. -- New York : Scherer, 1984.
Algebra and geometry / by Henry Fine. -- Bronx: Roux, 1982.

Some titles have subtitles. They consist of a title proper and a subtitle. By the *ALA Filing Rules* only the title proper is considered for filing. This can lead to complications. An alternate rule is suggested here: consider all that precedes the author statement to be the title:

Algebra / by Joe Doe. -- New York : Scherer, 1981.
Algebra and geometry / by Henry Fine. -- Bronx: Roux, 1982.
Algebra: Selected rules / ed. by Jane Sulk. Boston: Rausch, 1980

DIVIDED CATALOGS

The *ALA Filing Rules* of 1980 were designed for the so-called "dictionary catalog," a catalog wherein author, title, and categorical entries are arranged in one sequence. Some libraries find it helpful to arrange their catalog in two divisions (author/title and subject) or to divide it into three sequences (author, title, and subject). Filing into divided catalogs is simpler. Since all categorical added entries are filed separately, the question of context does not come up.

FILING OF CROSS REFERENCES

See references are filed by the same rules that apply to other entries. For *See also* references a special rule applies—they are filed ahead of their corresponding catalog entries:

JEWS
see also
ISRAELIS
JEWS
History of seven . . .

JEWS--BIOGRAPHY
Five masters of the . . .
JOBBERS
see
WHOLESALERS

LOCATION CODE OR "CALL NUMBER" FILING

The filing of books or shelf list cards by location codes is done as follows. The first step is to determine the file designation. A shelf list card marked "840 A2," for example, indicates by the absence of a special file designation that it belongs into the "stack" shelf list, the list of all books that reside in the regular book stacks. If the card were marked "REF 840 A2" instead, it would have to be filed in the "reference" shelf list. If marked "Oversize 840 A2" it would go into the "oversize" shelf list, and so on.

The second step in location code filing is the ordering by notation. This step varies somewhat depending on the classification or shelf location system used. Only the two major classification systems are considered here.

Dewey Number Filing

If the Dewey system is used, location code filing is first a question of numerical order. Here are two shelf list cards in order:

840
B9
845
A2

Decimal fractions, too, are filed numerically:

845.1
P6
845.2
M2

If the class symbols are alike in two compared codes, filing proceeds by the book symbols:

840
A6
840
B4

Should the compared book symbols begin with the same letters, filing is by the numerical part:

840
B3
840
B4

It should be noted that numbers in book symbols are considered decimals, not integers. The reason, of course, is that book symbols must be expandable to preserve the alphabetical order of the titles they represent, which can often only be achieved by interpolating a fraction between integers. This means that the numerical parts of two compared book symbols are evaluated as if they were preceded by decimal points. Here is an example:

840
H3
840
H35
840
H4

The decimal .35 is less than the decimal .4, which is why H35 comes before H4, as shown. Here is a comprehensive example with Dewey numbers:

840
A6
840
B3
840

B4
840
B9
840
H35
840
H4
845
A2
845
A2
B6
845.1
P6
845.2
M2

Library of Congress Symbol Filing

If the Library of Congress classification system, a mixed notation of alphabetical and numerical symbols, is used, filing is first a question of alphabetical order:

QD
11
S29
QE
6
A22

If the alphabetical symbols are equal in two compared codes, filing is by the numerical part of the notation:

Q
6
Z7
Q
11
A2

If the numerical part includes a decimal fraction, filing is still by numerical magnitude:

Q
10.8
T6
Q
11
S2

If the letters and numbers in the first two lines of a Library of Congress location code are alike, filing proceeds by the next part, which is almost always alphanumeric:

QD
11
R3
QD
11
S2

If the letters of that part of the code are alike, filing is by the numerical part, read as decimals:

QD
11
S29 (i.e., .29)
QD
11
S3 (i.e., .3)

A comprehensive example with Library of Congress codes follows:

Q QD
6 11
Z7 S29
Q QD
10.8 11

T6 S3
Q QE
11 6
A2 A22
Q QE
11 6
S2 A22
F5
QD
11 QE
S2 6
A3

Part III

USING THE COMPUTER

Chapter Fourteen

Doing Catalog Cards
with the Help of a Computer

Historically, library catalog cards were typed, one by one. Some libraries bought ready-made cards from the Library of Congress and other sources. Both methods are being phased out as we go from hand-typed or printed cards to cards run off from data stored in a computer.

No doubt some things change, but others don't. No matter how we do our cards, what does not change are the complexities of bibliographic description. Thus, there is still the question of the description principle: there are single-volume books that require only one main entry. Others come in sets of two or more volumes and may require several main entries. Also, a book still has to have a title. Some have subtitles. Sometimes the author is known, sometimes not. Some books have one author, some have several co-authors. Some require an entry for an editor. Some types of publications need an entry for a performer, a conductor, etc. Subject access is important, too. So are publisher, publication date, size of the book, etc. All of this detail still needs to be considered.

There are two important changes. The first is that once we abandon the typewriter in favor of a computer with card-producing software we need no longer concern ourselves with the layout of the various cards. The software "knows" how to do this. All we need to do is supply the data, the elements of bibliographic information that we used to type on the cards. The second change is that we need to supply this information only once. The computer does the rest.

But if the computer is to store all the elements of a bibliographic description and use them to print cards it must have the data in a format that adheres to a precise standard. Such a formatted record is divided into many clearly designated fields. To establish a new record the cataloguer enters each element—the author's name, the title, etc.—into the appropriate field.

There are many different software products on the market, of course. They all have at least one thing in common: they require data in a precise format. Formats vary in detail from system to system. It is not within the scope of this book to describe or evaluate all card production software packages. By way of example, though, we offer a brief sketch of one simple card writing program, The Librarian's Helper: A Productivity Tool for Librarians, by Jennifer Pritchett and Fred Hill, Version 5.0 for MS-DOS (Metuchen, NJ: Scarecrow Press, 1988).

The cataloguer who uses The Librarian's Helper to compose a set of catalog cards is presented with an input template that spells out 24 fields for bibliographic data. Not all of them are needed for every book, of course. For each book that comes up the cataloguer chooses from among them as required. Here is an annotated list of the 24 fields:

1. Author: The software was written to produce "standard" author main entry cards. For the production of title main entry cards this field must be ignored, left blank.
2. Title proper: This field is required. No card can be generated unless this field is present. All other fields are optional.
3. Subtitle and 4. Parallel title: Only occasionally needed.
5. Uniform title: This field is used for standard author main entries only. For title main entries that require a uniform title added entry use the added entry field (17).
6. Statement of responsibility and 7. Subsequent statement of responsibility: Name of the author(s), editor, etc. in the form in which they are given on the title page.
8. Edition: Best used only for editions other than the first.
9. Material specific details: Use for certain nonbook items like compact discs.
10. Place of publication: American libraries prefer a major American city if several are given.
11. Publisher: Name of publisher, omitting "Inc." and similar suffixes.
12. Date: Latest copyright date.
13. Call number: The system allows up to five lines.
14. Series note: Applicable only if book is part of an important or well-known series.

15. Tracings: This actually means "Subject headings." It is a repeatable field.
16. Analytical entries: For works within collections and anthologies. Up to ten title/author pairs can be entered.
17. Added entries: This actually means "Added entry headings other than subject headings." For title main entries, use these repeatable fields to enter all authors' names, in Last name / First name order.
18. ISBN and 19. Library of Congress number: International standard book numbers and Library of Congress control numbers are primarily used for item identification. Not very important for library patrons but sometimes handy for reorders.
20. Extent of item: Number of pages, volumes, etc. Important for positive identification.
21. Other physical details: Such as presence of illustrations, if deemed important for users.
22. Dimensions and accompanying materials: Height of book in centimeters, or note concerning medium such as "stereo, 4 1/2 inches."
23. Note paragraphs: Up to four paragraphs of notes are accepted. Use for important information that does not fit elsewhere and does not require a separate heading.
24. Shelf card information: Housekeeping information, not intended for the public.

Here is an example of a completed input template for a fictitious book:

AUTHOR	\<not applicable>
TITLE PROPER	Gardening by the foot
SUBTITLE	Box-grown veggies
PARALLEL TITLE	\<not applicable>
UNIFORM TITLE	\<not applicable>
STATEMENT OF RESPONSIBILITY	Jacob R. Mittleider
SUBSEQUENT STATEMENT OF R.	\<not applicable>
EDITION	2nd ed.
MATERIAL SPECIFIC DETAILS	\<not applicable>
PLACE OF PUBLICATION	New York
PUBLISHER	Pitman
PUB DATE	1993
CALL # 1	635
CALL # 2	M5

SERIES NOTE	<not applicable>
TRACINGS	Gardening
ANALYTICAL ENTRIES	<not applicable>
ADDED ENTRIES	Mittleider, Jacob R.
ISBN	0987654321
LIBRARY OF CONGRESS NUMBER	92030515
EXTENT OF ITEM	229 p.
OTHER PHYSICAL DETAILS	ill.
DIMENSIONS, ACCOMP. MATER.	25 cm.
NOTE PARAGRAPHS	Includes directory of box vendors
SHELF CARD INFORMATION	copy 1

When these data are provided The Librarian's Helper will generate a set of cards. They are first shown on the screen. At this point the cataloger has a chance to proofread and edit the cards. If all is found correct the printer is activated and the resulting error-free cards can be filed.

Here is a sample, the set of cards produced from the template shown above. The title main entry card looks like the card shown in Figure 85. Using the data given in the template the system generates an author card that looks like the card shown in Figure 86. In addition, the system will

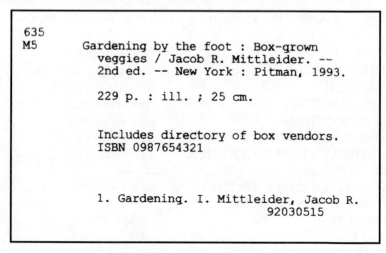

```
635
M5        Gardening by the foot : Box-grown
          veggies / Jacob R. Mittleider. --
          2nd ed. -- New York : Pitman, 1993.

          229 p. : ill. ; 25 cm.


          Includes directory of box vendors.
          ISBN 0987654321


          1. Gardening. I. Mittleider, Jacob R.
                                   92030515
```

Figure 85. *Title main entry card*

```
         Mittleider, Jacob R.
635
M5       Gardening by the foot : Box-grown
         veggies / Jacob R. Mittleider. --
         2nd ed. -- New York : Pitman, 1993.

         229 p. : ill. ; 25 cm.


         Includes directory of bax vendors.
         ISBN 0987654321



           1. Gardening. I. Mittleider, Jacob R.
                              92030515
```

Figure 86. *Author card*

```
         GARDENING
635
M5       Gardening by the foot : Box-grown
         veggies / Jacob R. Mittleider. --
         2nd ed. -- New York : Pitman, 1993.

         229 p. : ill. ; 25 cm.


         Includes directory of box vendors.
         ISBN 0987654321



           1. Gardening. I. Mittleider, Jacob R.
                              92030515
```

Figure 87. *Subject card*

generate a subject card that looks like the one shown in Figure 87. The shelf list card will look like the card shown in Figure 88.

One feature of The Librarian's Helper that may be particularly welcome in small libraries is the capability to create cards for up to ten

```
  635
  M5        Gardening by the foot : Box-grown
            veggies / Jacob R. Mittleider. --
            2nd ed. -- New York : Pitman, 1993.

            229 p. : ill. ; 25 cm.

  copy 1
            ISBN 0987654321



            1. Gardening. I. Mittleider, Jacob R.
                         92030515
```

Figure 88. *Shelf list card*

works contained in collections and anthologies. Such "analytics" make more work for the staff because they have to be filed, but they are of great help to patrons. The library may have only one version of Shaw's play "Pygmalion," for example, buried in a book called *Three Significant Plays of the World Theatre*. That play will be all but lost unless analytics are provided. Here are two cards that The Librarian's Helper will print out from information provided in the "Analytical entries" field of the template. The first is a title card filed under "Pygmalion," as shown in Figure 89. The second is an author card filed under "Shaw," as shown in Figure 90.

Similar cards would be printed for "Hamlet" and "Faust," of course. As was stated above, the limit is ten analytics, ten author/title pairs. But if a book should contain more than ten works for which the library wants to make analytics all is not lost. One of the great things about automation is that one can almost always outsmart the computer and make it do something for which it was not specifically programmed. In this case one simply creates separate brief records for the additional works. These records have only four fields: the title of the work, an added entry for the author, the call number of the book that contains the work, and a note explaining that the work is "In" a certain book. Figures 91 and 92 show two examples of such brief cards. One is for the title of a fictitious work, and the other is for the author of the work.

```
            Pygmalion
812             Shaw, Bernard
D7          Three significant plays of the world
            theatre / Edited by Joe Doe. --
            London : Dunk, 1999.

            300 p. : ill. ; 25 cm.


            Contains: Pygmalion, by B. Shaw. --
            Hamlet, by W. Shakespeare. -- Faust,
            by J. W. Goethe.
                ISBN 0123456789
                I. Doe, Joe. II. Author analytics.
            III. Title analytics.
                                    99230515
```

Figure 89. *Title analytic card*

```
            Shaw, Bernard
812             Pygmalion
D7          Three significant plays of the world
            theatre / Edited by Joe Doe. --
            London : Dunk, 1999.

            300 p. : ill. ; 25 cm.


            Contains: Pygmalion, by B. Shaw. --
            Hamlet, by W. Shakespeare. -- Faust,
            by J. W. Goethe.
                ISBN 0123456789
                I. Doe, Joe. II. Author analytics.
            III. Title analytics.
                                    99230515
```

Figure 90. *Author/title analytic card*

A word of caution: any tricks such as these need to be carefully thought through. There absolutely has to be a way to trace these extra analytics, for example, so that no blind cards are left in the catalog when the "Best shorter novels" book is lost or discarded. If the main entry for the book includes the full contents there will be no problem. If that is

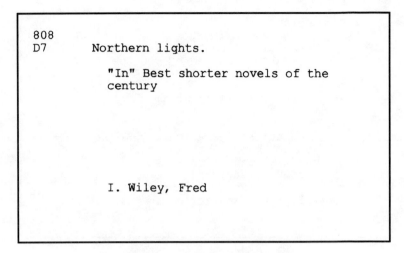

Figure 91. *Brief title analytic card*

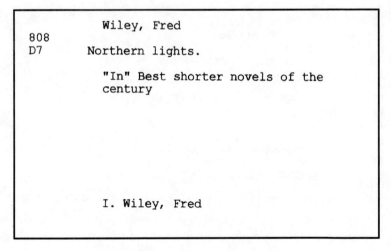

Figure 92. *Brief author analytic card*

not the case it would be advisable to either add the missing information to the main entry, or perhaps staple a Xerox copy of the contents page to the shelf list card.

A note on card stock. Pin fed card stock has a tendency to "hang up." One we have found very satisfactory is University Products' medium weight, LC cream, continuous catalog card.

Chapter Fifteen

Doing Away with Cards: The On-Line Catalog

As we have seen, the computer can simplify and speed up the production of cards. But cards still have to be filed by hand. This is costly in time and manpower. The card catalog is always subject to human filing error. More importantly, perhaps, each card can be filed in only one place, namely by the first word of the heading. The title card for *Every Autumn Comes the Bear* can be found only by looking under the first word, "Every." In a card catalog there is no access to any of the other words in the title.

However, when a library converts from a card catalog to an on-line catalog all this changes. There is no manual filing involved, hence no time wasted and no filing errors. The bibliographic data are entered only once, reducing the chance for typographic errors and such. Once the record is entered the on-line catalog software takes over. Vendors of software packages include programming that stores the record in such a way that the computer can access the data field by field. As a result, patrons may search for an author, a co-author, an editor, a performer, a title, a title keyword, a subject heading, a subject keyword, or any one of a number of other access points, or even combinations of access points such as author "and" title. When a search command is given the computer scans the appropriate fields. If a match is found in any of the records stored in the database the computer will display that record and show where in the library the item is located. In most library systems this screen display looks much like the catalog card of old, but that is where the similarity ends. The on-line catalog is a considerably more powerful retrieval tool.

SEARCHING THE BIBLIOGRAPHIC RECORD

To repeat, the significant difference between a card catalog and an on-line catalog, from the point of view of the library user, is the availability of access points. Potentially, the computer can be made to look at any field, and at any number of fields, and retrieve the records in which those fields are present. Not only can the computer be made to look at any field, but it can be programmed to look at every word, every "character string," in a given field. This gives the on-line catalog its keyword searching capabilities. If a book is entitled *Every Autumn Comes the Bear* it can be found by searching for the title word "every," of course. But a search for the words "autumn" or "bear" will also retrieve the book, a considerable increase in retrieval power when compared with the card catalog

A word of warning is indicated here, however. Keyword searches can retrieve many irrelevant items instead of, or along with the one that is wanted. A search for the keywords "Autumn" and "Bear" might retrieve the book entitled *Every Autumn Comes the Bear*. But it could also retrieve a collection of poetry, instead, entitled *Can Autumn Bear the Weight of Coming Winter?*

There is more. Depending on the software used, it may be possible to specify a subject heading "and" an author's name. This is referred to as a Boolean "and" search. We could say that such a search will retrieve everything on that subject by that author. That is not quite true, however. It will retrieve every record that has that subject heading in a subject field, and that author's name in an author field. And there is a difference. If, for example, a book contains contributions by two authors on two subjects, a simple Boolean search might well produce what is called a "false drop" because the computer cannot determine which subject goes with what author.

The same is true for author/title searches. Suppose the library has a book entitled *The Drug Dilemma*, edited by Warner. It contains, among others, Smith's essay "Drug abuse rehabilitation" and Jones' "Children and drugs." Jones has also written a book entitled *Rehabilitation and Drugs: A Handbook*, which the library does not own. It goes without saying, of course, that what the library does not have the on-line catalog cannot retrieve. But library users cannot know beforehand what the library has or does not have. So a patron looking for Jones' *Handbook*

might search for author "Jones" "and" keyword "rehabilitation" and retrieve Warner's *The Drug Dilemma* instead of Jones' *Handbook*. This
happens because in most on-line systems today the program would first
look for the author "Jones" and then for the title keyword "rehabilitation." If any record in the database has both words in searchable fields
the computer registers a hit. In this case the name "Jones" was found in
one field, the word "rehabilitation" was found in another field. The result is a false drop.

There are other ways to narrow a search, such as excluding material,
perhaps "everything on the subject of airplanes 'but not' military airplanes." In some systems searches can be limited by date (only newer
materials, or only older materials, as needed). Some on-line catalog
software systems allow "fuzzyness" when it comes to spelling. This is
helpful for the person who can't decide if it is "labor" or "labour," for
example.

If the indexing and retrieval functions are to work smoothly it is im-
perative that authors, titles, subject headings, etc. be placed into the correct fields. The computer is unforgiving in this respect. If the name of a
person functioning as author shows up in a subject field it cannot be retrieved through the author index, no matter how logical that would seem
to a human. The person in charge of catalog data input, therefore, must
be clear about the difference between an author ("this is a book *by*
Bernard Shaw") and a subject ("this is a book *about* Bernard Shaw"), or
a subject ("this is a book about cats") and a title ("this is a book entitled
Cats").

Software packages that rely on indexes to retrieve authors, titles, keywords, etc. may enable the library to establish an indexing profile. This
process requires the cataloguer to decide which fields to access by author, by title, and so on. Simpler systems offer a built-in, one-size-fits-
all profile. Other systems take a different approach to programming and
do away with indexes and profiles. To make it all run smoothly the cataloger must be cognizant of the way his or her system functions. If it is
desired to retrieve works by authors' names, for example, those names
must go into fields that the software treats as "author."

In addition to software—a system of programs that accept bibliographic data, store them, make them searchable, and display them on a
screen—an on-line catalog requires a certain minimum of hardware.
There has to be a server that stores the bibliographic data together with

the programs that make it all work, and there must be terminals for catalog input and for patrons to search the database.

LH ON-LINE: ON-LINE PUBLIC ACCESS CATALOG

There are many different software packages on the market today. They range from very expensive large-library systems that are capable of doing just about anything a library might want to make available to readers, all the way down to PC-based systems that are inexpensive but ipso facto limited in their capabilities. We offer here a brief description of one of these small menu driven library on-line catalog packages, LH On-line: On-line Public Access Catalog, version 1.0 for MS DOS, by Bob Pritchett, Jennifer Pritchett, and Fred Hill (Scarecrow Press, 1991).

Entering Data into LH ON-LINE

Inside LH On-line the bibliographic data are stored in different fields. They are the same fields The Librarian's Helper card program uses, discussed in Chapter 14. To begin data input the cataloguer calls up the system menu and selects the "Add a record" command. This brings to the screen successive input boxes or frames that are labeled with the field names. Some fields are indexed, which means that they can be searched. Others are not indexed, which means that their contents are displayed but cannot be searched. The fields are discussed briefly below.

Author (Indexed) The first input frame that comes up is labeled "Author." This sounds simple and self-explanatory, but note that the field allows for only one name. If a book has several authors, those names go into successive added entry fields. If the book in hand does not have an author the field can be left blank.

Title Proper (Indexed) The "Title Proper" field should be considered a required field. Although the system permits it, the field should never be left blank. Doing so invites trouble: a record without a title may be accepted by the computer but become irretrievable.

Subtitle (Indexed) This is often referred to as the "remainder" of the title.

Parallel Title (Indexed) Used in the rare situation when the title is given in different languages.

Uniform Title (Indexed)   Used when the item is a work that has appeared under varying titles and the goal is to catch all versions in one search. If one book is called *The Tragedy of Hamlet* and another is called *The Tragical History of Hamlet, Prince of Denmark*, and both contain the same play, it may be useful to add the uniform title "Hamlet" to both catalog records.

Statement of Responsibility (Not Indexed)   Name of the author, in straight order (first name, last name).

Subsequent Statement of Responsibility (Not Indexed)   Used in the rare situation when there is another person or group involved in an author-like capacity, such as a translator.

Edition (Not Indexed)   Can be ignored unless the item is known to be a second or subsequent edition.

Material Specific Details (Not Indexed)   Used for certain nonbook items such as video cassettes or compact discs.

Place of Publication (Not Indexed)   If more than one city is shown in the item, enter the first mentioned one. American libraries prefer an American city if one is named.

Publisher (Indexed)   Keep the name short: "Merriam" rather than "G. & C. Merriam Co., Publishers." Since the field is indexed it is important to be consistent: once G.& C. Merriam becomes Merriam it must always be entered as Merriam.

Date (Not Indexed)   It is best to enter the latest copyright date.

Call # (Indexed)   The system allows up to five lines.

Series Note (Indexed)   If an item is part of a series that the library's users might look for enter here the title of that series.

Tracings (Indexed)   A better term for this field would have been "Subject headings." The system allows up to ten lines of subject headings.

Analytical Entries (Indexed)   If an item contains many works, up to ten title/author pairs can be entered here. This is analogous to a table of contents.

Added Entries (Indexed)   This field is for co-authors' names, performers' names, and similar headings other than subject headings and analytics.

ISBN (Not Indexed)   If deemed important, enter the 10-digit international standard book number. Enter without hyphens.

Library of Congress Number (Not Indexed)   Like the ISBN, the Library of Congress control number is used primarily for identification in the ordering process. These numbers are of little use once the book is in hand.

Extent of Item (Not Indexed) Typically the number of pages or similar information.

Other Physical Detail (Not Indexed) Typically a note indicating that the book contains illustrations, if that is deemed important to library users.

Dimensions and Accompanying Materials (Not Indexed) Typically the height of the book or similar information. May also contain a brief note indicating that a booklet, a map, a diskette, or some other material comes with the item.

Note Paragraphs (Indexed) Up to four paragraphs of notes can be entered. Use for any helpful information that does not fit elsewhere.

Shelf Card Information (Not Indexed) This field is for housekeeping information such as "missing page 50" or "another copy in director's office" or such.

Indexing and Searching LH On-line

Once the cataloger has entered all available bibliographic data pertaining to a new book into their appropriate fields the new record is filed. At that point LH On-line software goes through an indexing cycle, marking the contents of all indexed fields for retrieval. This takes a few seconds per record and the result is a comprehensive keyword index.

As was indicated above, for the catalog user keyword indexes can cause problems. A person looking for the title "European architecture," for example, may well retrieve another book entitled "Modern trends in European architecture," i.e., a false drop. But in a small library the keyword index is probably satisfactory, especially when searches can be tailored to one's needs. In LH On-line one can search the comprehensive keyword index (all words in all indexed fields). But one can also restrict a search to one of five segments: authors, titles, subjects, notes, and publishers names.

LH On-line has another useful feature, the capability of combining terms by means of the logical operators "and," "or," and "not." These can be used in conjunction with the comprehensive keyword index or with the author, title, subject, publisher, or note segments. To elaborate on the example given above, if "European architecture" is by Smith and "Modern trends in European architecture" is by Jones, a search formulated like this:

T=European architecture (and) A=Smith

will retrieve the correct title (if it is in the collection), or will draw a blank (if the library does not have that book). Both results are correct in the specified circumstances, and the false drop is avoided. What LH On-line does not have is a truncation feature. Thus one cannot search for part of a word like "architect," hoping to catch all related terms such as architect, architects, architecture, architectural, and so on.

In addition to building a keyword index the LH On-line software also compiles two authority files, one for authors' names and one for subject headings. The purpose of the author authority file is to help the cataloguer prevent confusion and duplication of names. If the cataloguer enters an author as "Smith, John" one day, and "Smith J." the next, the machine assumes that these are different names. Searching for "Smith J." will not retrieve the book by "Smith, John." Thus it may be a good idea to check the authority file before entering a name. There is a problem, however. The author authority file is not complete. It is based on one field only, the author field. Names of co-authors, placed in added entry fields, do not appear in the authority file.

The subject authority field collects all headings entered into the tracings fields. The resulting list can be viewed on the screen or printed out. This makes the cataloguer's life easier should it become necessary to assign subject headings to a new book.

Another feature that the current version of LH On-line lacks is the capability to import or download records from bibliographic utilities such as OCLC. This and many other features are readily available in other, more complex systems, usually at correspondingly higher cost in money as well as in time to learn all the bells and whistles. This market is constantly in flux. Information about library software packages can be found on the Internet. A simple "Yahoo" search that we have found fruitful is "library services software." This search produces scores of vendor names with links to home pages, demo downloads, price lists, and more.

Chapter Sixteen

Downloading MARC Records from a Bibliographic Utility

Some library catalog software systems permit the downloading of bibliographic records from bibliographic utilities such as OCLC, RLIN, WLN, and others. Access to such utilities is by subscription or a contract which typically includes some instruction or a manual explaining how to search the database and locate records. The mechanics of downloading bibliographic records from the utility's database to your own catalog vary, of course, depending on which catalog software system your library acquired. Presumably your library catalog software vendor will have supplied a manual or a set of help messages to guide the operator from step to step.

Capturing existing catalog records from another database saves much decision making and keyboarding labor. The cataloger will find that all major bibliographic utilities store their records in what is known as the MARC format. MARC is the most widely used communications format for machine-readable catalog data. It is maintained by the MARC Standards Office at the Library of Congress. The format has fixed length fields as well as variable length fields.

Fixed length fields are control fields and fields that contain codes describing material and physical characteristics, transaction log information, and such. The actual meat of bibliographic description—authors, titles, subjects, etc.—is found in the variable fields. Each variable field consists of three parts: a tag, indicators, and subfields. Each field has a three digit numerical tag. Tag 245, for example, is the tag for the field that carries primary title information. Tag 300 holds the physical description of the cataloged item. Tag 650 is reserved for topical subject headings, and so on.

Most fields have one or more indicators. These are numerical codes that convey information such as the number of leading characters to be ignored in filing. If the second indicator in tag 245, for example, contains a value of "4" this tells the computer to disregard the first four characters, including the space. For a title like *The Way of All Flesh*, this means that it is filed under "W." If the indicator were to be given as 0 the title would be filed under "T" instead. Or worse, if the indicator for a title like "Academic success" is set at "4" the machine, not being able to think, will file the record among the e's for "emic success."

All fields have at least one subfield. Most subfields are designated by letters, beginning with "a." Some subfields have numerical designators or numbers. In field 700, for example, subfield #a contains a person's name, subfield "d" his or her dates, and subfield "4" may specify the person's function by a code such as "prf" for "performer." The complete description of all fields and subfields in its print on paper version requires two loose-leaf volumes of more than 1000 pages. Since the MARC format is primarily a communications format designed to convey the most complete possible bibliographic description of an item, and one cannot predict who in the library world may want what information at any given time, a specific field or subfield has been allocated to almost any bibliographic detail imaginable. However, the small library cataloger will need only a reading knowledge of the MARC language, so to speak. And for that purpose familiarity with a limited number of fields and subfields will do. Here is a list of some twenty MARC fields that the cataloger in a small library may have to decipher when trying to decide if an existing record found on-line in someone else's database fits a new book acquired by his or her library:

MARC TAG, MARC NAME, AND EXPLANATION

010   Library of Congress Control Number
Assigned to MARC records by the Library of Congress

020   International Standard Book Number
Assigned by the ISBN agency in New Providence, NJ

050   Library of Congress Call Number
Assigned by the Library of Congress to its own books

082   Dewey Decimal Class Number
Assigned by the Library of Congress for use by other libraries that
download MARC records

100   Main Entry—Personal Name
Actually the name of the principal person considered responsible for the
existence of the book. In card catalog terms, this is the "main entry
heading"

110   Main Entry—Corporate Name
Actually the name of the organization considered to be responsible for
the book

245   Title Statement
This is the most important of the MARC fields. In many on-line cata-
logs this is the only field that is required, all others being optional
Subfield #a: Title proper
Subfield #b: Remainder of title

246   Varying Form of Title
Another title for the same book that varies somewhat from the title
given in 245. May contribute to the further identification of the book

250   Edition Statement
Often used if book is not the first edition

260   Imprint
Contains facts of publication
Subfield #a: Place of publication
Subfield #b: Name of publisher
Subfield #c: Date of publication

300   Physical Description
Describes the item as a physical object
Subfield #a: Size of book—number of pages
Subfield #c: Size of book—height in centimeters

440   Series Statement—Title
Used if the book is part of a series

500   General Note
Helpful data that do not fit anywhere else

505   Formatted Contents Note
Contains full or partial, plain or enhanced, table of contents, depending
on the indicator settings

600   Subject Added Entry—Personal Name
Name of a person who is the subject of the book

650   Subject Added Entry—Topical term
Subject heading in the narrow sense, topic the book deals with

651   Subject Added Entry—Geographic name
Name of a country, city, etc. that is the subject of the book

700   Added Entry—Personal Name
Name of co-author, performer, editor, conductor, etc. not mentioned in
field 100

710   Added Entry—Corporate Name
Name of organization responsible for the book and not already mentioned in field 110

740   Related or Analytical Title
Title of a work contained in an anthology or collection described by the
title in field 245

Here is an example of a MARC record, simplified by skipping all but
one of the fixed fields:

008   #a920828s1993   nyu   j   000 1 eng
100 1 #aArnosky, Jim.
245 10 #aEvery autumn comes the bear /#cJim Arnosky.
260   #aNew York :#bPutnam's,#cc1993.
300   #a29 p. :#bill. ;#c29 cm.
650 0 #aBears#vJuvenile fiction.

In this record field 100 has a first indicator ("1") which says that the author's name is of the single surname variety (most names are). The name appears in its inverted form, last name first. There can never be more than one name in a field 100, and there can only be one field 100 in a record.

Field 245 has a first indicator ("1") which can be used to tell the computer that this record has a field 100, a bit of information that is of no interest to the cataloger. The second indicator in field 245 ("0") is more important. It tells the computer that there are no leading characters to be omitted in filing, or in other words, that the title does not begin with an article. Subfield #a contains the title of the book. Subfield #c shows the author's name in its uninverted form as found on the title page.

Field 650 has a second indicator ("0") which says that the heading is the one used by the Library of Congress. The subject heading shown here consists of a subfield #a for the topic "Bears" (the book is about bears) and a form subdivision #v indicating that this book is fiction for young people. Here is another MARC record:

```
008     #a870204s1987    couaf       00010 eng
020     #a0987654321
082     #a917.8
100 10  #aAnderson, Fletcher,#d1948-
245 10  #aRivers of the Southwest :#ba boaters guide tothe rivers of
        Colorado, New Mexico, Utah, andArizona /#cFletcher Ander-
        son and Ann Hopkinson.
246 33  #aBoaters guide to the rivers of Colorado, New Mexico, Utah
        and Arizona
250     #a2nd ed.
260 0   #aBoulder, Colo. :#bPruett Pub. Co.,#cc1987.
300     #a129 p. :#bill. ;#c21 x 26 cm.
650 0   #aRafting (Sports)#zSouthwestern States #vGuidebooks.
650 0   #aWhite-water canoeing#zSouthwestern States #vGuidebooks.
651 0   #aSouthwestern States#vGuidebooks.
700 10  #aHopkinson, Ann,#d1951-
```

This book has two authors. Their names are recorded in fields 100 and 700, respectively. Field 245 #a contains the title proper, as it is sometimes called. Subfield #b contains the remainder of the title or subtitle. Subfield #c holds the statement of responsibility as found on the title page. Field 246 contains the subtitle alone. It should be noted that, unlike field 245, MARC field 246 has no provision for character suppression. That is why the initial article has been omitted. There are two topical subject headings (650) in this record and one geographical one (651). Subject headings, including those shown here, are often subdivided. In the MARC format, topical subdivisions are designated as subfield #x. Chronological subdivisions are designated #y. Geographical subdivisions are designated #z. Form subdivisions are designated #v.

Field 082 contains a suggested Dewey class number. MARC records also have several fixed fields that serve a variety of purposes. In these examples we have shown only one of them, control field 008. It has 40 positions (0 to 39). In the case of the "bear" book shown above position 22 contains the code "j" which means that the book is meant for juvenile readers. Position 33 has the value "1" which tells a properly programmed computer that the book contains a work of fiction. Each of the other positions has a similarly precise meaning. The gaps, incidentally, are empty positions that contain nothing but are counted by the computer and are therefore as important as all other positions in the field.

The most important part of the downloading process is to decide if a record captured from a bibliographic utility and now showing on the screen fits the book in hand and should become one's permanent catalog record. Of particular use for this decision is field 020. When the ISBN is provided and matches the one in the book it is highly likely that the catalog record is a perfect fit. But one should always double check at least fields 245#a, 250, and especially field 300#a, the number of pages: if the number of pages shown in the captured record varies significantly from the book in hand, this may be a first indication of a discrepancy. The cataloger will then have to do some biblio-detective work, maybe some further database searching, until a more suitable record is found. Failing that, one will do best by settling for what was found, editing or modifying the record later.

Sometimes there are other problems. Here is an example. The book in hand has an ISBN but the record that matches lacks the 020 field. If your catalog is set up to allow searching by ISBN you should add the 020 field or anyone searching your catalog for the ISBN will miss this book.

Here is another example. The record that matches the book you acquired has the following subject heading:

Appalachian Mountains, Southern
#xSocial life and customs
#xStudy and teaching (Secondary)
#zGeorgia
#zRabun Gap

An elaborate heading like this is essential for organizing materials in a large library with thousands of books about the Southeastern states. But your small library has only half a dozen books about the Appalachians, if that many. Better to shorten the subject heading to:

Appalachian Mountains #xSocial life and customs.

It should also be pointed out that, depending on the system vendor's loading and display profile, the library's online catalog may not utilize certain fields or subfields. The MARC record might have, for example, an 830 field which, along with field 008 and some others, on downloading, simply "disappears." Many systems ignore the finer distinctions such as those indicated by subfields 650#x, #y, #z, and #v, which may affect the searching and display capabilities of the catalog. In some systems the cataloguer may well input certain data that show on the staff monitor but are suppressed from the public access catalog display. It is important that staff be aware of what the public sees as opposed to what the staff module and the MARC record show. A familiarity with MARC fields and their contents, and with the way they are processed for searching and display by your on-line catalog software, is the sine qua non for making it all work. There will be glitches, no doubt, and there is a learning curve, but after some practice and, one hopes, with the software vendor's support, the cataloger should have no major problems on downloading records from a bibliographic utility.

Appendix A

Examples of Catalog Cards

EXAMPLE 1

Figures 1a through 1f show a stand-alone work of type 1 with one personal author.

```
635
G2              Gardening by the foot : mini grow-boxes
                  for maxi yields / [by] Jacob R. Mitt-
                  leider. -- Bountiful, UT : Horizon
                  Publishers, 1981.
                  143 p.


1. VEGETABLE GARDENING.   2. CONTAINER GARDENING.
I. Mittleider, Jacob R.   II. Title: Mini grow-
boxes for maxi yields.
```

Figure 1a. *Main entry*

```
635              VEGETABLE GARDENING
G2              Gardening by the foot : mini grow-boxes
                  for maxi yields / [by] Jacob R. Mitt-
                  leider. -- Bountiful, UT :Horizon
                  Publishers, 1981.
                  143 p.
```

Figure 1b. *First subject added entry*

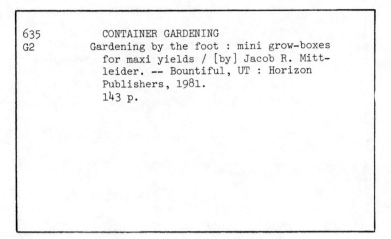

Figure 1c. *Second subject added entry*

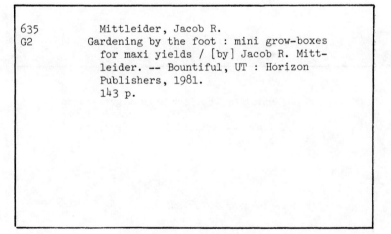

Figure 1d. *Author added entry*

```
635           Mini grow-boxes for maxi yields
G2            Gardening by the foot : mini grow-boxes
              for maxi yields / [by] Jacob R. Mitt-
              leider. -- Bountiful, UT : Horizon
              Publishers, 1981.
              143 p.
```

Figure 1e. *Title added entry*

```
635
G2            Gardening by the foot : mini grow-boxes
              for maxi yields / [by] Jacob R. Mitt-
              leider. -- Bountiful, UT : Horizon
              Publishers, 1981.
              143 p.


(space for housekeeping information...)
```

Figure 1f. *Shelf list card*

EXAMPLE 2

Figures 2a through 2f show a stand-alone work of type 1 with two personal authors.

```
692.1
R3          Reading construction drawings / Paul I.
            Wallach ; Donald E. Hepler. -- New
            York : McGraw-Hill, 1981.
            313 p.




1. SPECIFICATION WRITING.  2. BUILDING--CONTRACTS AND
SPECIFICATIONS.  I. Wallach, Paul I.  II. Hepler, Donald E.
```

Figure 2a. *Main entry*

```
692.1          SPECIFICATION WRITING
R3          Reading construction drawings / Paul I.
            Wallach ; Donald E. Hepler. -- New
            York : McGraw-Hill, 1981.
            313 p.
```

Figure 2b. *First subject added entry*

```
692.1           BUILDING--CONTRACTS AND SPECIFICATIONS
R3          Reading construction drawings / Paul I.
            Wallach ; Donald E. Hepler. -- New
            York : McGraw-Hill, 1981.
            313 p.
```

Figure 2c. *Second subject added entry*

```
692.1           Wallach, Paul I.
R3          Reading construction drawings / Paul I.
            Wallach ; Donald E. Hepler. -- New
            York : McGraw-Hill, 1981.
            313 p.
```

Figure 2d. *First author added entry*

```
692.1        Hepler, Donald E.
R3           Reading construction drawings / Paul I.
             Wallach ; Donald E. Hepler. -- New
             York : McGraw-Hill, 1981.
             313 p.
```

Figure 2e. *Second author added entry*

```
692.1
R3           Reading construction drawings / Paul I.
             Wallach ; Donald E. Hepler. -- New
             York : McGraw-Hill, 1981.
             313 p.



(space for housekeeping information)
```

Figure 2f. *Shelf list card*

EXAMPLE 3

Figures 3a through 3f show a stand-alone work of type 1 with one corporate author and several personal authors.

```
624.2
G9          Guide for the field testing of bridges /
               prepared by the Working Committee on
               Safety ; B. Bakht [et al.]. -- New
               York : American Society of Civil
               Engineers, 1980.
               72 p.


1. BRIDGES--TESTING.  I. American Society of Civil
Engineers. Working Committee on Safety.  II. Bakht, B.
```

Figure 3a. *Main entry*

```
624.2       BRIDGES--TESTING
G9          Guide for the field testing of bridges /
               prepared by the Working Committee on
               Safety ; B. Bakht [et al.]. -- New
               York : American Society of Civil
               Engineers, 1980.
               72 p.
```

Figure 3b. *Subject added entry*

```
624.2        American Society of Civil Engineers.
G9           Working Committee on Safety
          Guide for the field testing of bridges /
          prepared by the Working Committee on
          Safety ; B. Bakht [et al.]. -- New
          York : American Society of Civil
          Engineers, 1980.
          72 p.
```

Figure 3c. *First author added entry*

```
624.2        Bakht, B.
G9        Guide for the field testing of bridges /
          prepared by the Working Committee on
          Safety ; B. Bakht [et al.]. -- New
          York : American Society of Civil
          Engineers, 1980.
          72 p.
```

Figure 3d. *Second author added entry*

```
624.2
G9              Guide for the field testing of bridges /
                prepared by the Working Committee on
                Safety ; B. Bakht [et al.]. -- New
                York : American Society of Civil
                Engineers, 1980
                72 p.



(space for housekeeping information...)


```

Figure 3e. *Shelf list card*

EXAMPLE 4

Figures 4a through 4d show a one-volume collection of articles, a book
of type 2, with one person named as editor.

```
136.7354
A4              Adolescent : a book of readings / edited
                by Jerome M. Seidman. -- Rev. ed. --
                New York : Holt, 1960.
                870 p.




1. ADOLESCENCE.  I. Seidman, Jerome M., ed.


```

Figure 4a. *Main entry*

```
136.7354    ADOLESCENCE
A4          Adolescent : a book of readings / edited
            by Jerome M. Seidman. -- Rev. ed. --
            New York : Holt, 1960.
            870 p.
```

Figure 4b. *Subject added entry*

```
136.7354    Seidman, Jerome M., ed.
A4          Adolescent : a book of readings / edited
            by Jerome M. Seidman. -- Rev. ed. --
            New York : Holt, 1960.
            870 p.
```

Figure 4c. *Author added entry*

```
136.7354
A4        Adolescent : a book of readings / edited
          by Jerome M. Seidman. -- Rev. ed. --
          New York : Holt, 1960.
          870 p.




(space for housekeeping information)
```

Figure 4d. *Shelf list card*

EXAMPLE 5

Figures 5a through 5g show a one-volume collection of papers presented at a meeting, a book of type 2, with two editors.

```
574.19
P6        Photoreception and sensory transduction /
          edited by Francesco Lenci and Giuliano
          Colombetti. -- New York : Planor Press,
          1980.
          422 p.

          Papers presented at the Advanced Institute
          of Photoreception, Versilia, Italy, 1979.

1. PHOTORECEPTORS.  2. SENSES AND SENSATION.  I. Ad-
vanced Institute of Photoreception, Versilia, Italy,
1979. II.Lenci, Francesco. III. Colombetti,
Giuliano.
```

Figure 5a. *Main entry*

```
574.19        PHOTORECEPTORS
P6         Photoreception and sensory transduction /
              edited by Francesco Lenci and Giuliano
              Colombetti. -- New York : Palnor Press,
              1980.
              422 p.
```

Figure 5b. *First subject added entry*

```
574.19        SENSES AND SENSATION
P6         Photoreception and sensory transduction /
              edited by Francesco Lenci and Giuliano
              Colombetti. -- New York : Planor Press,
              1980.
              422 p.
```

Figure 5c. *Second subject added entry*

```
574.19     Advanced Institute of Photoreception,
P6         Versilia, Italy, 1979
           Photoreception and sensory transduction /
             edited by Francesco Lenci and Giuliano
             Colombetti. -- New York : Planor Press,
             1980.
           422 p.
```

Figure 5d. *First author added entry*

```
574.19     Lenci, Francesco
P6         Photoreception and sensory transduction /
             edited by Francesco Lenci and Giuliano
             Colombetti. -- New York : Planor Press,
             1980.
           422 p.
```

Figure 5e. *Second author added entry*

```
574.19      Colombetti, Giuliano
P6          Photoreception and sensory transduction /
              edited by Francesco Lenci and Giuliano
              Colombetti. -- New York : Planor Press,
              1980.
              422 p.
```

Figure 5f. *Third author added entry*

```
574.19
P6          Photoreception and sensory transduction /
              edited by Francesco Lenci and Giuliano
              Colombetti. -- New York : Planor Press,
              1980.
              422 p.


(space for housekeeping information...)
```

Figure 5g. *Shelf list card*

EXAMPLE 6

Figures 6a through 6c show a one-document collection or recorded musical pieces, an item of type 2, with one person named as performer.

```
AUDIO
          Virgil Fox playing the organ at the
          Riverside Church. -- [New York] : RCA,
          [1950]
          Sound disc : 33 1/3 rpm, mono. ; 12 in.

          RCA Victor LM 2268


I. Fox, Virgil.
```

Figure 6a. *Main entry*

```
AUDIO     Fox, Virgil
          Virgil Fox playing the organ at the
          Riverside Church. -- [New York] : RCA,
          [1950]
          Sound disc : 33 1/3 rpm, mono. ; 12 in.

          RCA Victor LM 2268
```

Figure 6b. *Author (performer) added entry*

```
AUDIO
            Virgil Fox playing the organ at the
            Riverside Church. -- [New York] : RCA,
            [1950]
            Sound disc : 33 1/3 rpm,mono. ; 12 in.




(space for housekeeping information...)
```

Figure 6c. *Shelf list card*

EXAMPLE 7

Figures 7a through 7e show a special issue of a periodical that contains one work, an item of type 3 cataloged under the document description principle, with one personal author.

```
336.2
M5          Mineral severance taxes in Western States :
            economic considerations / Sandra Black-
            stone. -- Golden : Colorado School of
            Mines, 1981.
            39 p.

            Colorado School of Mines Quarterly, v. 75,
            num. 3, ISSN 0010-1753

1. MINES AND MINERAL RESOURCES--TAXATION--THE WEST
I. Blackstone, Sandra. II. Title: Colorado School
of Mines Quarterly, v. 75, num. 3, July 1980.
```

Figure 7a. *Main entry*

Appendix A

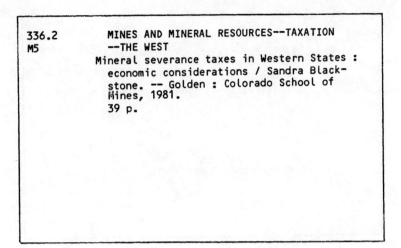

```
336.2      MINES AND MINERAL RESOURCES--TAXATION
M5         --THE WEST
           Mineral severance taxes in Western States :
           economic considerations / Sandra Black-
           stone. -- Golden : Colorado School of
           Mines, 1981.
           39 p.
```

Figure 7b. *Subject added entry*

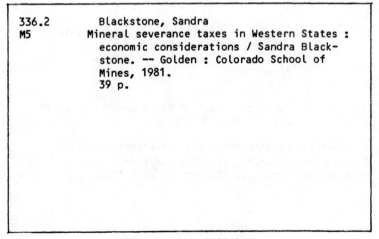

```
336.2      Blackstone, Sandra
M5         Mineral severance taxes in Western States :
           economic considerations / Sandra Black-
           stone. -- Golden : Colorado School of
           Mines, 1981.
           39 p.
```

Figure 7c. *Author added entry*

```
336.2        Colorado School of Mines Quarterly,
M5           v. 75, num. 3, July 1980.
             Mineral severance taxes in Western States :
               economic considerations / Sandra Black-
               stone. -- Golden : Colorado School of
               Mines, 1981.
             39 p.
```

Figure 7d. *Connective added entry (set title)*

```
336.2
M5           Mineral severance taxes in Western States :
               economic considerations / Sandra Black-
               stone. -- Golden : Colorado School of
               Mines, 1981.
             39 p.


(space for housekeeping information)
```

Figure 7e. *Shelf list card*

EXAMPLE 8

Figures 8a through 8f show an issue of a periodical that has its own document title, an item of type 6 cataloged under the document description principle, with one editor.

```
320.05
P7            Police and violence / special editor
                 Lawrence W. Sherman. -- Philadelphia :
                 American Academy of Political and
                 Social Science, 1980.
                 211 p.

                 Annals of the American Academy of
                 Political and Social Science, v. 452,
                 ISSN 0002-7162

   1. POLICE--UNITED STATES.  2. VIOLENCE--UNITED STATES.
   I. Sherman, Lawrence W., ed.  II. Title: Annals of the
   American Academy of Political and Social Science, v. 452.
```

Figure 8a. *Main entry*

```
320.05        POLICE--UNITED STATES
P7            Police and violence / special editor
                 Lawrence W. Sherman. -- Philadelphia :
                 American Academy of Political and

                 Social Science, 1980.
                 211 p.
```

Figure 8b. *First subject added entry*

```
320.05        VIOLENCE--UNITED STATES
P7            Police and violence / special editor
              Lawrence W. Sherman. -- Philadelphia :
              American Academy of Political and
              Social Science, 1980.
              211 p.
```

Figure 8c. *Second subject added entry*

```
320.05        Sherman, Lawrence W., ed.
P7            Police and violence / special editor
              Lawrence W. Sherman. -- Philadelphia :
              American Academy of Political and
              Social Science, 1980.
              211 p.
```

Figure 8d. *Author added entry*

```
320.05        Annals of the American Academy of Political
P7            and Social Science, v. 452
              Police and violence / special editor
              Lawrence W. Sherman. -- Philadelphia :
              American Academy of Political and
              Social Science, 1980.
              211 p.
```

Figure 8e. *Connective added entry (set title)*

```
320.05
P7            Police and violence / special editor
              Lawrence W. Sherman. -- Philadelphia :
              American Academy of Political and
              Social Science, 1980.
              211 p.




(space for housekeeping information)
```

Figure 8f. *Shelf list card*

EXAMPLE 9

Figures 9a and 9b show a periodical, an item of type 7. Housekeeping information is kept on a special periodical check-in card and there is no shelf list.

```
              Journal of earth. -- New York :
              American Earth Society, 1984-

              v. 1, num. 1-

              Quarterly



I. American Earth Society.
```

Figure 9a. *Main entry*

```
              American Earth Society
         Journal of earth. -- New York :
              American Earth Society, 1984-

              v. 1, num. 1-
```

Figure 9b. *Author added entry*

EXAMPLE 10

Figures 10a through 10e show a two-volume work, a book of type 8, with one editor.

```
621.48
R4          Research, training, test, and production
            reactor directory / Reed Burn, editor ,
            S. Krapp, project manager. -- La Grange
            Park, IL : American Nuclear Society,
            1980.
            2 v. (1922 p.)




1. NUCLEAR REACTORS--UNITED STATES.   I. Burn, Reed.
II. American Nuclear Society.
```

Figure 10a. *Main entry*

```
621.48       NUCLEAR REACTORS--UNITED STATES
R4           Research, training, test, and production
             reactor directory / Reed Burn, editor ;
             S. Krapp, project manager. -- La Grange
             Park, IL : American Nuclear Society,
             1980.
             2 v. (1922 p)
```

Figure 10b. *Subject added entry*

```
621.48      Burn, Reed
R4          Research, training, test, and production
            reactor directory / Reed Burn, editor ;
            S. Krapp, project manager. -- La Grange
            Park, IL : American Nuclear Society,
            1980.
            2 v. (1922 p.)
```

Figure 10c. *First author added entry*

```
621.48      American Nuclear Society
R4          Research, training, test, and production
            reactor directory / Reed Burn, editor ;
            S. Krapp, project manager. -- La Grange
            Park, IL : American Nuclear Society,
            1980.
            2 v. (1922 p.)
```

Figure 10d. *Second author added entry*

```
621.48
R4          Research, training, test, and production
            reactor directory / Reed Burn, editor ;
            S. Krapp, project manager. -- La Grange
            Park, IL : American Nuclear Society,
            1980.
            2 v. (1922 p.)


(space for housekeeping information)
```

Figure 10e. *Shelf list card*

EXAMPLE 11

Figures 11a through 11f show an item of type 5, a set of books in which each book has its own distinctive title. One of the three books of the set is cataloged under the document description principle. A work analytic has been made for one of the essays contained in the volume. Compare with example 12.

```
QE
39          Ocean floor / ed. by Hamdy Bolles. --
0 3             New York : Bagsby, 1980.
                540 p.

            The Oceans, v. 2



1. SUBMARINE GEOLOGY.  I. Bolles, Hamdy, ed.
II. Title: Oceans, v. 2.  II. Ewing, Thomas.  Structure
of the Gulf of Mexico, in
```

Figure 11a. *Main entry*

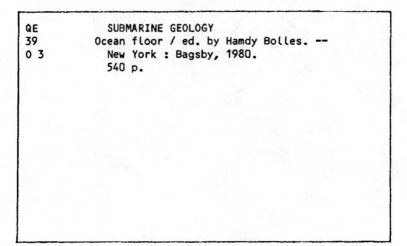

Figure 11b. *Subject added entry*

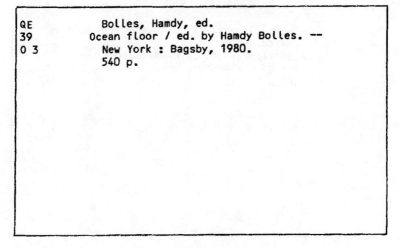

Figure 11c. *Author added entry*

Appendix A

```
QE              Oceans, v. 2
39              Ocean floor / ed. by Hamdy Bolles. --
0 3             New York : Bagsby, 1980.
                540 p.
```

Figure 11d. *Connective added entry (set title)*

```
QE              Ewing, Thomas.  Structure of the Gulf of
39              Mexico, in
0 3             Ocean floor / ed. by Hamdy Bolles. --
                New York , Bagsby, 1980.
                540 p.
```

Figure 11e. *Author and title work analytic*

```
QE
39          Ocean floor / ed. by Hamdy Bolles. --
0 3           New York : Bagsby, 1980.
              540 p.




(space for housekeeping information)
```

Figure 11f. *Shelf list card*

EXAMPLE 12

Figures 12a through 12h show an item of type 5, a set of books where each book has its own distinctive title. The item is cataloged under the set description principle. One work analytic has been made for one of the essays contained in volume 2, and book analytics have been made for the three component volumes. Compare with example 11.

```
GC
57              Oceans / ed. by Hamdy Bolles. --
0 3                 New York : Bagsby, 1980.
                    3 v.

                    Contents: v.1. Sea water -- v.2. Ocean
                    floor -- v.3. Ocean currents


1. OCEANOGRAPHY.  I. Bolles, Hamdy, ed.  II., III., and
IV. Title analytics as in contents note.  V. Ewing, Thomas.
Structure of the Gulf of Mexico, in v.2 of
```

Figure 12a.   *Main entry*

```
GC              OCEANOGRAPHY
57              Oceans / ed. by Hamdy Bolles. --
0 3                 New York : Bagsby, 1980.
                    3 v.
```

Figure 12b.   *Subject added entry*

```
GC              Bolles, Hamdy, ed.
57              Oceans / ed. by Hamdy Bolles. --
0 3             New York : Bagsby, 1980.
                3 v.
```

Figure 12c. *Author added entry*

```
GC              Sea water, v.1 of
57              Oceans / ed. by Hamdy Bolles. --
0 3             New York : Bagsby, 1980.
                3 v.
```

Figure 12d. *First book analytic*

```
GC            Ocean floor, v.2 of
57            Oceans / ed. by Hamdy Bolles. --
0 3           New York : Bagsby, 1980.
              3 v.
```

Figure 12e. *Second book analytic*

```
GC            Ocean currents, v.3 of
57            Oceans / ed. by Hamdy Bolles. --
0 3           New York : Bagsby, 1980.
              3 v.
```

Figure 12f. *Third book analytic*

```
GC              Ewing, Thomas.  Structure of the Gulf of
57              Mexico, in v.2 of
0 3          Oceans / ed. Hamdy Bolles. --
             New York : Bagsby, 1980.
             3 v.
```

Figure 12g. *Author and title work analytic*

```
GC
57           Oceans / ed. by Hamdy Bolles. --
0 3          New York : Bagsby, 1980.
             3 v.


(space for housekeeping information)
```

Figure 12h. *Shelf list card*

EXAMPLE 13

Figures 13a through 13d show a kit consisting of five pieces, with only one author traced.

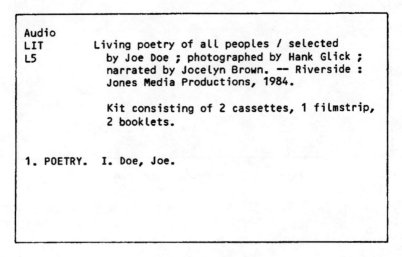

Figure 13a. *Main entry*

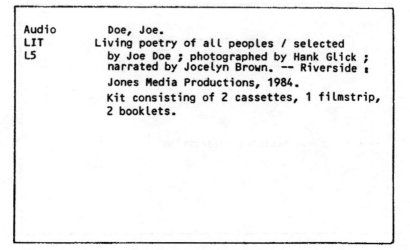

Figure 13b. *Author added entry*

```
Audio        POETRY
LIT          Living poetry of all peoples / selected
L5               by Joe Doe ; photographed by Hank Glick ;
                 narrated by Jocelyn Brown. -- Riverside :
                 Jones Media Productions, 1984.

                 Kit consisting of 2 cassettes, 1 filmstrip,
                 2 booklets.
```

Figure 13c. *Genre added entry*

```
Audio
LIT          Living poetry of all peoples / selected
L5               by Joe Doe ; photographed by Hank Glick ;
                 narrated by Jocelyn Brown. -- Riverside :
                 Jones Media Productions, 1984.
                 Kit consisting of 2 cassettes, 1 filmstrip,
                 2 booklets.


(space for housekeeping information)
```

Figure 13d. *Shelf list card*

Appendix B

Library Supplies and Equipment

Wherever books and other publications are cataloged and prepared for use, certain supplies and equipment are needed. Several nationwide distributors specialize in this market. Here are the addresses of some well-known firms:

Brodart Co.
500 Arch Street
Williamsport, PA 17705
www.brodart.com

Demco, Inc.
Box 7488
Madison, WI 53707
www.demco.com

Gaylord Bros.
Box 4901
Syracuse, NY 13221-4901
www.gaylord.com

Highsmith, Inc.
W5527 Hwy 106
PO Box 800
Fort Atkinson, WI 53538-0800
www.highsmith.com

University Products, Inc.
517 Main Street
Box 101
Holyoke, MA 01041-0101

These firms issue profusely illustrated catalogs, many of them on the Web, that also convey a good bit of practical, technical information. Here is a selected list of some of the supplies and equipment a small library might require:

Accession sheets
Adhesive tape
Adhesives ("library paste")
Book cards and pockets for check-out
Book covers, clear plastic
Card catalog cabinet
Card sorter
Cassette albums
Catalog cards, 7.5 × 12.5 cm
Catalog cards, continuous form, pin fed
Catalog guide cards
Charging trays
Charging tray guides
Dictionary stand
Electric eraser
Erasing fluid or tape
Marking stylus
Message labels (e.g., "For Room Use")
Microfilm storage cabinet
Pamphlet binders
Paper cutter
Periodical checking cards
Princeton files
Rubber stamps
Self-adhesive labels
Sign marker
Slide sorter
Stapler, heavy duty
Typewriter with card holder (to prevent smearing of cards when typing near the edge)
Visible record cabinet for periodical checking cards